# Backstage

# Backstage

## How I Almost Got Rich Playing Drums in a Christian Hardcore Band

Aaron Lunsford

Editor: Matt Johnson

Copy Editors: Abigail Pruss & Matt MacDonald

Cover Design: Caitlin Thompson

Published by: BC Words

2015

First Printing: 2015

BC Words

www.badchristian.com

www.aaronlunsford.com

ISBN 13: 9780692494608 (BC WORDS) (PAPERBACK
ISBN 10: 069249460X

# Dedication

To Cassie, Magnolia, and Buddy

# Table of Contents

# Acknowledgements

A big thanks to Matt Carter for encouraging me to continue writing this book after sending him the first couple chapters on a whim. Thanks to my editor, Matt Johnson, for knowing what it's like to have your knuckles bleed from behind a drum kit. Abigail Pruss & Matt MacDonald, my copy editors, thank you for allowing me not to sound like the uneducated southerner band dude that I am. Also thanks to other BC folks that took the time to read and critique along the way - Simon, Nick, others that I am forgetting or find too insignificant to mention. Of course, thanks to my wife Cassie for allowing me to tarnish our family name with my foul mouth and sour attitude.

To my band:
I'm not going to sit here and gush about camaraderie and brotherhood and the "community" that I am constantly being bombarded with from the millennial church culture of 2015. Being in a band was and is hard. I've made it hard. My bandmates, Cody, Colin and TJ made it hard at times. But damn, we are all still friends, 12 years after I joined As Cities Burn. That's a fucking accomplishment worth ACKNOWLEDGING.

# | 1 |
# This Is It

**It's August of 2006** and I'm in New Orleans. It's hot, and humid. Really humid. The type of humidity where you forget what the point of showering is. I'm just a sweaty, sticky mess. Rapidly accelerating my dehydration is the fresh Abita Amber - a local Louisiana beer - I just picked up from a bar across the street from the venue. I'm now enjoying it as I watch the openers load their gear in through the stage door. In New Orleans, it always seems like a good idea to start drinking early, despite the fact that in the morning you may have to get on a plane, or take a ride across Lake Pontchartrain on the 25-mile causeway back to the North Shore. Blowing chunks of jambalaya and hurricanes on that stretch of road is tough, seeing as there's no shoulder to pull over onto. But it's the last show of tour and my band, As Cities Burn, is headlining the House of Blues in New Orleans for the first time. We are on the verge of greatness. Riches and fame are inevitable. Abita Amber is the only appropriate action to take.

If I had only known the truth in that moment, sipping my beer, watching my friends in Jonezetta load their gear through the back entrance of HOB on Decatur Street, that THIS was as big as it gets. By the time As Cities Burn would come to an end in 2009, I would be humbled and broken, devastated by the suicide of a friend, a failed marriage, and the collapse of my band. No ill-advised night of drinking in New Orleans could match the metaphorical hangover that my life would become.

It was actually supposed to be our last show ever at the end of a very successful farewell tour. Bands are very narcissistic about their "farewells," aren't they? It can feel quite presumptuous to think that anybody is going to give a shit about your LAST TOUR EVER. Which, of course, it wasn't. As you may have noticed I wrote 'supposed to be our last show'. Turns out that "Farewell Tour" billing is worth a lot of tickets and a lot of merch sales and a lot of fans spilling their hearts about how important you are to their existence. This all must have been very convincing because about halfway through our "final tour" we decided to announce that in fact it was not! We had been so inspired by all the heartfelt gratitude from our fans (and their money) we realized what a stupid idea it was to break up. Besides, we were going to be HUGE once we put out our next record. That was the trajectory we were on. All the other bands on our label were blowing up at the time and we were next in line, so "they" said. We had the right booking agent. We had the right sound. We were getting the good tours. And the fans were damn passionate about what we were doing. There was a connection between As Cities Burn and the fans that was unexplainable. That connection exists to this day I believe. The Force is strong in our fan base.

We had to stay together. For the greater good of music, right?

───────────

This last show at House of Blues in New Orleans was kind of a dream come true for us. Just one year before we were still playing churches and VFW halls in our hometown. Headlining HOB was a rite of passage for us. It meant we were moving on to bigger and better things. I remember that night we believed we had a very good chance at selling out the show. I don't remember the capacity at the time, but I think the room could fit close to 1,000 people. It might be less now, but let's say 1,000. That sounds better than 878. So we were expecting 1,000 kids to come to this show. Sure, about 163 of them were friends and family but that's the way it always was when playing South Louisiana. All the members of the band besides myself were from nearby Mandeville and Covington, just across the lake, and also attended LSU before dropping out to tour full-time. They were popular guys and really fun to be around, so there were always people hanging wherever they were.

If you sell out a show at HOB New Orleans you get your name on the wall backstage. I remember being so giddy about the possibility of our band name written on a wall next to Jimmy Eat World and Foo Fighters. We were at the peak of our career, and on the verge of attaining the unattainable for a hardcore band from Baton Rouge, where frat-rock rules all and Zydeco country music is a real thing that people want to listen to. I dare you to Google "Zydeco".

As Cities Burn had survived dealing with shady local promoters and playing for free at churches. No longer did we have to work our asses off to promote and sell tickets for shows that we would receive no financial gain from, even though our draw was double that of the touring "national" act. We had arrived. We were legit:

"Pay us our money or we take a walk to the ATM buddy! And by the way we requested BUDWEISER, not Bud Light on the hospitality rider. FIX IT NOW!!!"

Truth is we were never like that. Never demanding. Never really that professional. We never took what we were doing too seriously. I think we were mostly surprised that this plan had worked. Dropping out of college and just hitting the road with no help whatsoever. We were surprised and proud. Excited for the future. In the end, our turn to blow up and become the next Tooth and Nail/Solid State Records screaming band to sell 100,000 records or more would never come. We had reached the peak and didn't have a fucking clue.

You see, we would end up changing genres completely. TJ, our singer/screamer, decided to leave the band, start a normal life and get married. Although we loved TJ we thought, "Well, now at least we can write the music we want to write and be part of the cool rock and roll indie scene." Cody, TJ's brother, would become our singer and As Cities Burn completely reinvented itself. Artistically, it was for the better. Our second and third records were much more in line with the type of music we all actually loved to listen to. But career-wise, it was devastating. Our sophomore release would end up selling half as many records as the first.

The shows got smaller. The booking agent was gone. The label loved the record, but it was like marketing a whole new band. Half of our fan base left us. Can't blame them. They liked screaming and hardcore dancing and moshing. You can't expect an 18-year old kid, whose existence is defined by wearing girl jeans and black t-shirts, to within a year become a thoughtful indie rocker. I was cocky about our transition. I thought that our music would have more mass appeal, and that we were going to be the biggest band in our "scene". Not even close.

  After our third record was released in the spring of 2009, the band was basically in shambles. We played one show in support of the record with no mention to anybody that it could be our actual last show. We were still friends, but relationships were strained. There was plenty of blame to go around, including myself. I was on the tail end of an eventual failed marriage that had deeply affected friendships and even my commitment to the band. At times I was selfish: missing practices, bailing out on shows, asking the band to tailor everything to my schedule. Oblivious to what was going on around me, my dream was falling apart and I didn't do a damn thing to try and save it.

That summer Cody posted on Facebook that the band was done, thanking the fans for six years of ACB support. None of us even discussed it. But someone needed to say something. So that was it.

---

Let's get something straight about this book. I'm not writing this about those years after our peak. That's a story for another time. I only mention that part of our history to give you context. This is a band that fell short in a lot of ways. Nobody bought houses with the money we made, so in that sense, there was really nothing material to show for it in the end. The financial success was minimal. We fell short of virtually every expectation I had on that hot August day in 2006.

Most of this book will be about three of the best years of my life, which also happen to be the beginning of three more years of absolute misery. Even though As Cities Burn embarked on a great adventure from 2003 to 2006, this time period was not without tragedy. Suicide. One could never imagine how many life trajectories can be jolted from their previous path due to the tragedy of suicide. I will write about these things with transparency. Because these things are all too intertwined with my experience in As Cities Burn.

I think in some ways this book is a way for me to appreciate that time in a way I was never able to back then. When you are always looking forward to what is next, it's difficult to live in the moment and realize how amazing those experiences are. With touring and trying to push your career forward, you're always thinking about where the next show is, how many tickets have been sold, are we going to get an offer for that amazing tour, how much merch we should re-order. Always looking forward to the next thing. Never enjoying what's happening to you right now.

Even with all the terrible things that would occur in my personal life, I want to enjoy those moments now. I want to tell you what it was like to come up as an indie hardcore band in 2003, before the internet took over every aspect of the music industry. I want to tell you what it's like playing for absolutely nobody in Brighton Beach, NJ, with a foot of snow on the ground awaiting you after the show as you search for a place to lay your head. I want to tell you about the overwhelming joy that you experience when you find out you sold more than $300 worth of t-shirts! Or the numbness and disappointment you feel when you mail over 100 press kits to record labels, managers and agents and don't receive a single response. These were the realities of starting out as a touring band in 2003. Maybe this is still true for 2015. I wouldn't know. I don't want to know. Well, not by way of experience that is.

Maybe this book will be a cautionary tale to some young, hopeful musicians who just know they can make it if they try! Or maybe somebody in their early 30's who had dreams of playing in a band and going on tour but never did will feel eternally grateful towards their younger selves that they decided to stay in college and become an engineer. Or maybe some of my peers will read this and declare that I am totally full of shit and starving for attention in my musical "twilight" years where I can no longer make a living doing what I love—that I just can't hack it in this business and that I am now trying to make a quick buck, exposing and exploiting things I know about the music industry and "Christian" bands.

My honest to God hope regarding the quality and success of this endeavor is that I just want my wife to like it and maybe laugh a few times. Dammit. That's a lie and I know it. I want to sell 100,000 copies and be the voice of a scene and generation of music fans that started underground and slowly made their way into the mainstream. I want to get fucking rich and be a panelist on Dr. Drew or Dr. Phil or Oprah or something, and talk about how "difficult it is for touring bands to maintain their mental and physical health on the road" or some bullshit.

Outside of trying to get rich and become a famous author, I think this is a story worth telling. But also, this band has real fans, and these fans might actually find this book interesting! Beyond that I hope that this story can appeal to someone who has never even heard of As Cities Burn. I really don't want this book to be *about* As Cities Burn. I hope fans of the indie/hardcore/Warped Tour scene in general can find entertainment in this book.

My intention is not to create a biographical account of our experience. I plan on writing hardly anything personal regarding the other band members. This is just my perspective of what can happen when kids dare to dream. You could change the band name and it wouldn't matter. If I wanted to please our fans I would leave out the chapter where I basically talk shit about our fans for 3,000 words. But it's relevant to this story. To *my* story.

This book is meant for those who long to see how this works from the inside: a firsthand account of an amazing experience by the drummer that fans still don't recognize even when he's wearing his own T-shirts left over from tours past. This happens a lot; "Hey, is that an As Cities Burn shirt??? Cool! What's your favorite record?" a kid asked me at the Whole Foods meat counter yesterday. Oh…and yes I wear my own band's T-shirts. I'm old; it doesn't matter.

I think it's possible for non-fans to read and enjoy this. Maybe this book can lead to new fans even. We are on the internet. Some interesting and amazing things happen when some 19-21 year old kids leave college to hit the road. To those who are not familiar with this world, it could seem like a crazy fantasy novel or something. Others may be appalled at the complete disregard for responsible adult behavior. "How do you pay bills?? Where do you live?? What are you going to do when you have a family one day?" Oops.

Whoever you are, if you like music I hope you find some level of enjoyment in reading this. And during the parts of the book that are dark and depressing, I hope you are able to find comfort and maybe allow these stories to relate to your own life in a meaningful way. Outside of poverty, suicide, and divorce, being in a band is really fun. We had lots and lots of fun. We lived in a fantasy world, a boys' club of sorts. It was an escape from all the bad stuff. And if you keep having fun for long enough, eventually the beer is free!

When I think about myself at 23 years old, sipping that Abita Amber, getting my mind ready for what I thought would be the ride of a lifetime, I wonder if it would have been better to know that the summer I had just experienced was as good as it would ever get for As Cities Burn. Would I have taken the time to enjoy it more, or been riddled with anxiety and feelings of let down and failure? It's probably wise to submit to the brilliance of Garth Brooks' "The Dance" on this matter. Yes, I like Garth Brooks, and I was in a post-hardcore band. Garth said he was "glad he didn't know, the way it all would end, the way it all would go." That's deep, Garth. I have to agree. If I had known on that day what I know now I probably would have drank too much and had to endure that awful trek across the lake, puking out the window at 55 mph.

Now, at 32 years old with a wife and two kids, I'm able to look back and appreciate it all. The good, bad and the ugly. In the summer of 2006 I was a dumb-ass, 23-year-old boy. No 23-year-old boy could possibly appreciate that experience the way he should. The way the experience deserved to be appreciated. Now I can. And now, I can write about it.

# | 2 |

# Lacking Confidence

**I first came to know about** As Cities Burn in February of 2003 when I attended a show in Ruston, LA, with my friend Tim Jordan. He was getting ready to fill in on guitar later that spring for a North Louisiana emo band called Rivers Indiana that was also playing that night. We made the drive from Arkadelphia, AR—where I was going to college at the time—to catch their set and hang out. I remember feeling very out of place at this show. All the guys were wearing tight jeans and t-shirts that let the top of their hips show. All the girls were cute with tattoos and cool haircuts. I was wearing some sort of Ralph Lauren button-down dress shirt left over from high-school-douchebag-jock days, trying to look nice, as I had high hopes of meeting a girl every single time I went out in public. This mentality created a tremendous amount of stress and social anxiety, a common theme throughout this book.

When ACB came onto the stage to set up—when I say stage I mean a six-inch platform at the Louisiana Tech Methodist Student Union or something—I could immediately tell there was something different about them compared to all the local bands back in central Arkansas. For one, they just looked cool. There was a feeling in the air that something interesting was about to happen. The anticipation coming from the crowd was something I had never witnessed toward a local band. It was like these kids knew something I didn't.

They started into their first song with deafening feedback that dropped out just as the two guitarists screamed an alternating vocal intro; "I COULD BE ONE OF THEM IF I DIDN'T FEEL SO ALONE!" then the other, "I COULD BE ONE OF THEM IF I DIDN'T FEEEEL!!" and then straight into a sick guitar riff, reeking of discord and emotion. This type of guitar work wasn't represented by local bands back home. This was different. They all had their backs to the crowd. Even the singer. They were loud. They were tight. They were like the best local band I'd ever seen.

On the next song, a much heavier one, they start throwing their guitars around their bodies only to catch them and have their fingers slide perfectly back to the chord they had just left. The whole band would recklessly fling their bodies all over the stage barely missing each other's faces on every pass. There was head banging and total disregard for the risk of damaging their equipment and each other. The audience was captivated in a way I had not witnessed in my local scene. It was some badass shit.

None of this was part of my reality in Arkansas. It wasn't even that I loved the music. I had rarely been a fan of heavy music. But I could just tell there was something special going on. Something unfamiliar to my life experiences thus far. I played in pop punk and ska bands throughout high school and into college. But this shit had substance and passion that I had not yet tapped into. I went home discouraged that night. Discouraged that I wasn't anywhere close to as cool as everything I had just witnessed. My friend Tim, the coolest guy in the room, went home with a girl's phone number.

---

A couple months later Tim calls me on his way back from Baton Rouge, having just played with Rivers Indiana. The show was with As Cities Burn at a backyard BMX rally. Tim's report included details about shitloads of kids connecting with the music, breaking into mosh pits and jumping off of roofs. He too had never seen kids react this way to a local band.     Tim was 6 foot 4, good looking and charismatic. He was a great first-impression-type of guy who always dominated whatever situation he was in, so it was no surprise when he told me that As Cities Burn tried to recruit him to be their drummer, as theirs was quitting very soon. But alas, Timothy did not play the drums. So whom did he tell them about? His less cool, shorter, confidence-lacking best friend, Aaron. Next thing I know we are planning a trip back down to Baton Rouge for my audition.

Once again, social anxiety takes over and I am pretty much miserable the entire weekend of my hangout and audition with the band. I've never been to Baton Rouge and it is undeniable that South Louisiana is like no other place in the country. Everybody was loose. The girls oozed sexuality. The presence of LSU and its party atmosphere was felt far and wide, whether you were partying or not. It's not the Bible belt down there. Arkansas is very conservative. I grew up Southern Baptist where basically everything fun was bad. Not that I hadn't broken free a little bit from that. After all, I had gotten my ears pierced when I turned 18! And I cursed like a sailor. Not very Southern Baptist of me.

But in Louisiana, land of excess and indulgence, I was a fish out of water. I could sense the skepticism from the band. I didn't look or even seem as cool as they did. And I wasn't making up for any physical shortcomings with my personality. I totally clammed up. But Tim, the epitome of cool and confident, was there by my side and for some reason he was vouching for me with these guys. That had to go a long way.

Being the popular guys that they were, people were always coming and going from their apartment—even if they weren't home. The ACB guys all lived together in a two-bedroom apartment with a loft. The exiting drummer was in the process of moving out and I hardly saw him, which was fortunate because it was an awkward situation for me, coming down there to try and be the new guy. A dude they called Fat Tony lived upstairs in the loft. He's the one who organized the crazy backyard BMX show—in their own backyard—and also served as the band's graphic designer and de facto sixth member. The dishes in the sink were piled high, a foot above the sink rim. Trying to move a dish was a death sentence, as the aroma coming from underneath was what I imagined the inside of a dead elephant's colon smelled like. Nevertheless, I thought—Hey! This seems fun!

Rehearsals that day were whatever. It wasn't really a style of music I was good at. The songs were structured loosely, with tempos changing constantly and lots of screaming. But they wanted to tour. Every single member of this band was committed to dropping out of college and hitting the road ASAP. The plan was to build up the bankroll around town for the summer and then in the fall leave town and never look back. I informed them that I had in fact been on tour before and even booked shows out of town. Turns out I was the most experienced touring musician in the room. This seemed to add to my value, which at that point must have been right about zero. Thank God for my pop punk band's summer tour the previous year that totally destroyed my Chevy Blazer.

On the second night I was in town, they called up a bunch of friends and decided we should go to the top of the abandoned Jimmy Swaggart building. Jimmy Swaggart was a big time televangelist, and apparently, a corrupt one. Big surprise, huh? Back in 1989 he started building this dormitory for his campus in Baton Rouge. But construction stopped and it was still just sitting there, totally empty and unfinished in 2003 and for many years after that. So naturally, kids used to sneak in and drink and have sex and do dumb stuff. Not us, but maybe other kids. We crawled under the fence and started making our way up this concrete block of nothing. I don't even think we had flashlights. And hardly anybody had cell phones back then. It was just...dark. The only light coming in was that of the moon and streetlights down below. It just seemed like a bad idea and one that I was not too thrilled about. Day two, and I was uncool AND a pussy. Not to mention I was extremely out of shape, seeing as how my diet at the time consisted of Cheez-Its and sweet tea.

However, once we made it to the top I could see the appeal of this endeavor. An amazing 360 view of the city, and with Baton Rouge being so flat, this meant you could see for miles. There was a sense of freedom and community up there, and a collective attitude of 'who gives a shit if we get caught.' I knew then that I wanted to be a part of this. These people were exciting. Climbing up on top of abandoned buildings, putting on backyard hardcore shows, throwing guitars around their necks. I felt that if given the opportunity, it was time to do something crazy. Even though it was scary to think about leaving behind every person I knew and cared about, in that moment I realized if I was ever going to make it, I needed to get out of Arkansas and take a risk.

Another thing playing in my favor was the fact that Cody (the main songwriter and lead guitarist/backup singer) and I kind of hit it off in terms of artistic vision. We had some great discussions about influences and philosophy on building songs and vibes. I was amazed at his talent and the ease in which his hands and fingers glided across the strings and fret board. He told me he was actually a bass player and had only taken up guitar a couple years before. I knew there was something special about this kid. I had no idea he would end up being the most talented, creative and one of a kind musicians I would ever come across. Much of the reason I had faith that As Cities Burn could do well was because of what I saw in him. Even though the demos were kind of shitty and the songs were all over the place, with time I knew Cody was going to develop into a badass. I was right, by the way.

I was packing my things, preparing to head back to Arkansas, and the guys hadn't broached the subject of evaluating the weekend. I figured maybe they wanted to spend a few days talking about it or even try out other drummers. I figured I probably didn't get the gig, because I definitely wasn't cool enough.

Maybe it was something Tim said or simply the fact that he was putting in the time to be my wingman on this quest. I wouldn't be surprised if Tim pulled the guys aside and said, "He may not seem like much, but you should give him a chance. This dude is dedicated and wants this as bad as y'all do," or something in that vein. Whatever the reason, just minutes before Tim and I began our five-hour trip back to his lake house in Camden, AR, the guys asked me to come outside the apartment into the driveway and offered me a spot in the band.

Actually TJ, the main singer/screamer wasn't out there. He was inside eating Chinese food. Mere seconds after I accepted the offer to join, TJ walks outside and says to his brother, "Hey Cody, check out my fortune...'Learn a new language, gain a new life'." He laughed and walked back in the house. We loaded up and headed home. Notably, Tim left town that night with a girl's phone number... again.

Before I had gone down to audition, I had just gotten a summer job in Cabot, AR at the local video rental store. I told the guys I would work that job for a month, save up some cash, and move down at the end of May. I wasn't sure exactly how much cash I would actually be able to save at $6.50 an hour for ten hours a week, but dammit that was my plan. A few days after I got back to Arkansas I decided that plan of action was foolhardy and I loaded up my Blazer with everything I owned (a drum set, clothes, TV and a Band of Brothers DVD set), went out to dinner with my parents to let them know I was moving to Louisiana that very night. Oh, and dropping out of college.

I was off. No shit, I didn't even tell any of my friends. I just left and would end up making phone calls over the next few days to inform people things like, "By the way, I won't be moving into that house with you next semester." The night before I decided to run off in haste, I had hung out with a few people at an All American Rejects show in Little Rock. They were playing Juanita's[1], which was a 400 cap room with amazing vibes and an amazing sound system. All American Rejects had already sold a million records probably, but for some reason were doing a small club tour. I only bring them up specifically now, because they will be a player throughout this book, a somewhat significant one in fact.

Tim and I were showing some friends the demos for

---

[1] *The original location on Main St. is kind of in a shady part of Little Rock. It has since moved downtown to the River Market District into a room with much less character and charm. But my favorite bar, Midtown, is still over by the original location. They are open till 5 a.m. if you ever need to party after the party.*

the bands we were joining. Tim, almost simultaneously to me, had landed a spot in a really good pop punk band from Northwest Arkansas called Welton. I could tell nobody liked what they were hearing of As Cities Burn. They knew I was moving soon to join this band and I'm assuming they couldn't figure out why. I guess my friends lacked the vision to spot the diamond in the rough. Well, everyone except Tim.

———————

Things weren't easy at first in Baton Rouge. I had no money. Meals consisted of PB&J and Kraft Mac & Cheese. For a splurge we might hit up Jack in the Box or Raising Canes. And the humidity? I was not ready for it. I couldn't breathe when I walked outside, and I'm not sure what caused it but I broke out in hives after being down there for a week. It rained every single day. Sleeping was tough: I shared a room with Colin, guitarist and kind of the band leader/personality, and the dude snored like crazy. Still does.[2] And of course you are sweating, because that's what you do in Louisiana. Sweat all day and all night.

I was able to land a job at the Tinseltown USA movie theater. TJ had applied to work there and received a call to schedule an interview. After some thought I guess he decided that he wasn't interested in tearing tickets so he told me to just go to the interview in his place. They were con-

———————

[2] *In later years on the road I would spend many nights sleeping alone in the van due to the insane snoring habits of my fellow band members.*

fused, but I got the job. It felt nice to get something going for income and I think the guys were impressed I took initiative to find employment so quickly as their previous drummer seemed to be notorious for a somewhat laissez faire existence. Sometimes you just gotta show up. Anyways, who cares about a dead end job? I moved here to bust ass playing shows and booking a tour. And that's exactly what we did.

One of the coolest things about looking back on this time is getting to recount the second show I ever played with As Cities Burn. In early June of 2003 we made the quick trip over to Gulf Port, MS. Back then I thought this whole part of the country was an absolute shithole. Now the gulf coast is my favorite place to be. But across the shithole we went and at that show we would meet two bands from Jackson, MS that would have major influence over our career and also become great friends, Jonezetta and Fletcher. Fletcher would several years' later change it's name to Colour Revolt and take the indie world by storm. If any of you reading this are fans of Brand New and the sound they ripped off—I mean matured into—on "The Devil and God Are Raging Inside Me"—you have Colour Revolt to thank for that. A couple years later, Jonezetta would end up signing one of the biggest record deals in Tooth and Nail history for a new band, as well as bringing my friend Tim on as a band member.

Every show we played that summer was insane from my perspective. I went from being in bands that hardly anyone cared about to being in a band that was the best draw in the scene. I witnessed hardcore dancing for the first time. I thought it was weird and stupid back then just as I do now, but the kids loved it. We even featured fans "dancing" in a DVD set to a Sigur Rós tune—lots of head banging and guitar throws with pretty music over it. We were certain that this DVD would set us apart, showcasing to labels that we really knew how to "throw down." It didn't.

The "throwing down" as we called it wasn't always a good thing in my opinion. I wanted to put on a good show, but I also wanted to actually play the songs. One show in particular where I found this to be an issue was in late summer of 2003. We were opening a show at a local Baton Rouge church for two touring bands. One was This Runs Through from North Carolina. Their singer Spencer would go on to join a group from Florida called Underoath. The other was, Evelyn, whose drummer and guitarist would go on to join Between the Buried and Me. Shane, guitarist for Evelyn, would years later help start a band we were good friends with - Oh, Sleeper. Weird how far back friendships can go. I say all this to make the point that these bands were good. They were on a noticeably different level at that time. A level I wanted to be on. But what happened at that show would prove to me that we had a long way to go.

In the midst of our normal "throwing down" throughout the set, there was a moment where I questioned exactly what we were even doing. I'm going along, playing my drum parts and as I look up I see our bassist, Pascal, throwing his bass 20 feet in the air over and over. I look to stage left and see Cody doing guitar throws around his shoulder using the strap, eventually descending down his arm like a hula hoop. So to be clear...also not playing his instrument. Then Colin, attempting the same trick as Cody, accidentally propels his guitar high into the air and off the stage into the crowd, crashing down and hitting a girl in the head. At that moment I was the only one playing an instrument. And I thought, "Are we even a band right now?"

We had been sending out press kits to every label under the sun. They were nice too. Very well put together due to Fat Tony's access to the LSU print shop. We thought for sure this would get us noticed. We even included that fancy Sigur Rós DVD along with our new demo. Hell, I dyed my hair black to keep in line with the image we were pitching: hard, tough, black hair dudes…wearing girl jeans.[3] We throw down, bitch. After many late nights researching where to send our press kits and hundreds of dollars of postage, we received our reward. Zero responses. Not even a single "Not Interested." We thought we were ready, but we weren't. And the industry knew it. Maybe they saw potential somewhere like I did, but it wasn't enough to even garner a response.

I think the show with the guitars flying into the crowd should have been a big enough indicator that we lacked seasoning. However, we were determined, and kids down in Baton Rouge cared about our band. We had great confidence that we could take this thing somewhere. So as was intended when I joined the band, we made plans to get

---

[3] *Just in case you don't know, wearing girl jeans somehow became a thing in the hardcore/indie scene back in the early 00's. I don't know why. I just did. I conformed. It was really uncomfortable for the crotch area in all honesty.*

out of Louisiana and tour. A lot. The booking of our first tour would begin and it would be on me to get it done. Foolishly, I volunteered to take it on alone as I of course had "been on tour" and had "lots of contacts." Twenty years old, inexperienced and stupid, I sent my band off into a brutal circuit of financial uncertainty and shows with nobody in attendance. Sound fun? Only for a band of hopeful idiots.

# | 3 |
# Fools On The Run

**Booking a tour is hard work.** Although booking agents have massive databases of promoter and venue contacts as well as software that streamlines the process of creating all the paperwork necessary for a tour, it's still hard. There are so many factors to consider; so many schedules to work around; so many different people you are in contact with all at once. In addition, the agent has to deal with all of the ridiculous requests and complaints from the artist about how a tour is shaping up. If not careful it can be what one might refer to so elegantly as…a clusterfuck. Booking, man. It is really hard and a huge pain in the ass, even for the pros.

An indie hardcore band trying to book their own tour in 2003 is akin to someone under 6-feet tall trying to play in the NBA. Sure, there are a few of those guys, but its just not very likely that it will work out for a player that size.

It's not that booking your own tour was impossible, there was just very little likelihood of it working out to where you don't lose your ass and end up stuck 2,000 miles away from home with no money to fill up the gas tank.

We didn't know this. A band of dreamers, I guess. Or maybe we did know and we refused to accept it. Remember how I said we received zero response from labels regarding our demo? That was a motivating factor for us. We'll show them what we are capable of; then the labels will take notice and offer us record deals galore. Because we had heard from other signed bands we opened for that hard work was the most attractive thing to a label. It's much easier to get behind a band that will put in the work on their own and get out on the road before anybody is helping them. But we were clueless as to how long we would have to grind it out on our own.

The booking process starts on the internet. In 2003 pretty much every venue had a website that would list their calendar and specific instructions regarding how to go about booking a show. The instructions were different for touring bands compared to locals. First, you must send in your press kit and demo. Without this there was no consideration whatsoever. No mp3s sent via email would be accepted. The instructions always had some self-righteous declaration about how "if you can't take the time to follow these instructions then you don't deserve to play" or some other bullshit. The thing was, every venue had different rules you had to follow; so keeping up with it all was mind-boggling.

I had this notepad that I was routing the tour on and would make notes next to every city specifying the venues I was attempting to book and the requirements to solicit them for a show booking. Some venues had specific hours that you must call on a specific day of the week. And if you didn't get a chance to call them or failed to get a hold of them during that time, then that was it. The instructions explicitly stated that calling for booking outside of those hours was frowned upon and may affect your chances of getting a show. Everyday I would have to check and see what venues I was due to call and plan my day around that.

Hardly anybody wanted to book through email, which is so insane looking back. Now hardly anybody wants to get on the phone, ever. Email is so efficient and I remember being so frustrated that more people weren't taking advantage of it. When I was able to get someone on the phone the conversation would often go like this:

Me: "Hey this is Aaron from As Cities Burn. How you doing?"

Venue: "What date are you looking to book?"

Me: "Ummm, either September 27, 28, or 29."

Venue: "Ok I'm not booking that week until next week so call back then." He hangs up.

One week later...

Me: "Hey this is Aaron from As Cities Burn again, I spoke with you last week about booking September 27, 28, or 29."

Venue : "Ah yeah, sorry man I already filled those dates."

Me: "You piece of shit."

Ok I didn't really say that. But that's how I felt. The process was ridiculous. However, it weeded out the ones not willing to do the work. Every once in a while I would get lucky and get the talent booker on the phone in a good mood. They pull your press kit out of a pile and for some reason agree to put you on a show with a bunch of locals so people will actually be there. It's a small victory, but it's an amazing feeling as you start to slowly fill up your calendar with confirmed tour dates. We didn't even care if they were paying us or if the show is literally in a garage. It's a show! There could be people and maybe even free pizza!

Through perseverance and blind luck, I was able to string together a few weeks of a tour up the East Coast into New England and back down through the mid west. Life on the road is a very difficult thing to describe. For one thing it's extremely boring. Most of your time is spent riding in a van or waiting for your turn to perform. When you are poor and have no idea when or what you will eat next, it can be a little maddening. Our band budget for meals was $3 per person. Which basically meant three items from the dollar menu at McDonalds. Finding a dollar on the ground meant your meal for after the show just became the envy of your band mates. Two double cheeseburgers, fries AND a soda? That was luxurious, my friend.

TJ created what we referred to as a "Sillypack." Don't ask me what the name means, because I don't remember and I can't imagine that it really means anything. Out there, shit gets weird and you come up with weird shit to get through it. A Sillypack was a small Tupperware container that would fit under your seat in the van. It was used to store your food supply. One would be allowed to get your $3 allotment per meal and put it towards a bulk purchase of foods to keep in your Sillypack. We had our staples like PB&J or maybe tuna and crackers for some of the more disgusting members of the band. I for some reason would always keep a bag of those Chinese La Choy noodle crackers to stuff my face with. But the best concoction to come out of a Sillypack was the pizza sandwich. Store brand white bread, spaghetti sauce out of a jar, and those little packets of pepperonis. Starting a band sound fun yet?

Entertainment consisted of Halo multiplayer in the conversion van and a football tossing game in Walmart parking lots. One guy would take a shopping cart and push it imitating a wide receiver; then the guy throwing would try to make it inside the moving target. There was no reward for winning. It was just something to do. We probably watched "Casino" ten times on that first tour. It was the only movie we had for the van's VHS player and since it was three hours long it passed the time well.

Cody would sometimes play 'Splinter Cell' on Xbox although with such a small screen in the conversion van, it could be difficult to see your enemies. The best place to sit while using the Xbox was most definitely the "captains" seats in the middle row of the van. There were no wireless controllers back then so if you were trying to sit in the back row to play, it really meant you were sitting on your knees leaning in towards the middle of the van so that your chord didn't get ripped out in the middle of a firefight. Didn't make it any easier that multiplayer Halo on our little TV meant that you had about 3 square inches dedicate to your sector of the screen. Being assigned to driving duty while Halo was being played was downright depressing. It would have doubled well as punishment for misbehaving crew members - if we could have afforded one that is.

———————

The shows…weren't good. Of course there was always the pleasant surprise of meeting local bands with weird schticks or band names. Mini Band in Delaware for instance played miniature instruments. Why? I do not know. Holy Shit was another band at that exact same show in Delaware. We played with a band named Holy Shit. To this DAY, that is still my favorite band name ever and I have often considered starting a band under that moniker.

I'm sure we gained a few fans on the tour and met plenty of nice people who fed us a hot meal and let us sleep on their floors, but it was mostly a bust. Plenty of shows cancelled. We made our way up to Boston only to have nowhere to play due to cancellations. So we hit the internet and started looking for shows to jump on. Pascal, our bassist, found a music festival that was open to letting us come do our set. We showed up and it was a Rockabilly festival and vintage car show. In case you missed it, we were a hardcore, screamo, something-or-other band. We decided it was best to take the day off.

The next day we were able to land a gig in western Mass-achusetts that sounded somewhat promising. The venue was a shed, but I'm not sure it was called "The Shed." It was way out in the middle of nowhere. Very *Children of the Corn*. It was fall so it was quite beautiful, but eerie. The leaves were changing colors, country roads and farmhouses filled the terrain, typical for what one would envision for that part of the country in the fall. But something about the wind and the fading sunlight made it all feel strange, like the beginning of a horror movie. When we arrived we were greeted by the very soft spoken show organizers who possessed a creepy disposition about them. They issue us name tags. Yes, name tags, and then proceed to make sure we help ourselves to some Boca Veggie Burgers. We debated whether or not to ditch this show as well, but it was almost a two-hour drive to get there so we figured what the hell.

We started setting up our merch, which in hindsight was totally pointless seeing as how those in attendance were likely against any form of commercialism or profits of any kind. When the first band started playing we knew we had made a mistake coming there. The show was for "noise" bands. Meaning there was no structure or rhyme or reason. The drummer was fat with rosy cheeks, dressed in a sailor outfit but without the shirt. This band was quite literally making up their songs as they went along. As was the crowd with their dancing, swaying and flinging their arms while rolling their eyes into the back of their head, looking towards the sky as if worshipping a God unbeknownst to me. The God of Noise, I presume.

When we played, the looks we received were mirror images of the looks we had on our faces during the other bands. WE were the weirdest people there in their opinion. Our songs had lyrics that were sung and screamed, and sometimes those lyrics and melodies were repeated! It was some wild shit for them to witness I am sure.

The headlining band performed out of their VW van. I can't remember what they were called, but they recently had an HBO documentary made about them. It seemed that they were the noise band equivalent of U2. The biggest noise band in all the land. The "singer" had a backpack with a fan attached that he would use to enhance their performance with pyrotechnics. The fan would turn on and propel bottle rockets and burn sparklers. Don't worry, the drummer was safe behind him because he was set up IN the van. I have never seen or heard of anything like this since that day. We hastily packed up our T-shirts and CDs and headed back to civilization. No sales were made that day.

Throughout our career the Northeast would never be too kind to us. While in New York City for the first time, after hours of trying to find somewhere to park our van and trailer, we made our way to The Bronx. Yes, you read that right. We thought, "Hey, lets go park our van and trailer with everything we own in one of the toughest neighborhoods in the country."

Upon finding a spot we were greeted by some young fellas playing basketball who wanted to welcome us to the neighborhood "Where you guys from? What you doing in New York? You leaving your car here overnight?" We answered all these questions honestly and unsuspecting. We even made sure to seek out their advice whether or not it would in fact be safe to leave our van there.

"OH YEAHHHHH!!! We'll keep an eye on it for you guys ya know?"

Off we went on the subway back to the Upper East Side, to stay with a friend from New Orleans who was living in the city at the time, excited and grateful to have found a safe and legal place to park our rig. The next day, when I went back to The Bronx to attend a Yankees doubleheader, I was assigned with the mission to check on the van before I came back into Manhattan. Windows broken, CD player gone, among other things. We was just dumb southerners, I guess. Although maybe they was dumber, because they didn't take any of our instruments that were just sittin' inside our rinky dink trailer.

After a few more shows of the promoters being completely M.I.A.—as in, yeah come play this show on this date, at this place...and then upon arrival there is no sign of a show to be found—and a blizzard in Ohio, we made our way back home. Somehow we had broken even on the tour. This was a great success and a miracle.

I have to admit that there was some tension when shows would fall through. It was hard not to get discouraged, and because I had taken on the task of booking the entire tour myself, there was some frustration cast in my direction.

But after realizing how naive we were to think that we should have expected anything more from that first tour, we decided to tackle the next one as more of a group effort so the blame could be shared among more than just one member of the band. Since we had the desire to head west, we decided that TJ would be in charge of booking all of the western U.S. shows and I would focus on the eastern part of the country. I even made us Yahoo email addresses to sound more legit.[4] Fight Club was still a big deal around this time and one of our favorite movies to watch. As lame as it was, we came up with "The Durden Agency."

After a few regional shows around the south and some holiday touring with our buddies in Fletcher, Rookie of the Year, and The Spill Canvas that covered the gulf coast and Birmingham, Jackson, and Monroe, we geared up to take on our longest stretch of touring to date. Three weeks touring the East Coast straight into a three-week West Coast leg. The first leg of the tour was a joint effort with Welton, the band from Arkansas that my BFF Tim had joined. We pretty much talked every day while I was on the road; so getting to go on a tour and actually hang out everyday was super cool to us.

---

[4] *My strange addiction—email addresses. I love creating new email addresses. I've probably made 15 new email accounts in the past four years. I come up with a business or blog idea or blog, create an email address and possibly a WordPress, and bam! It's a success. How could it not be if I have a new email address? Take a guess how many of those businesses and blogs I followed through on....*

Tim was a big fan of As Cities Burn. Always very encouraging to us and, in particular, Cody. Almost like it was his mission to not allow Cody to forget how special his talent was. I think he always hoped there would be a way for him to join the band. Even though I had only been in As Cities Burn for about seven months, I could already tell that Pascal, our bassist, was somewhat of an outsider. Like he just didn't click with the group.

It was cordial between everyone, but a lot of times there is always that one guy in the band that everyone seems to have issues with. Some small, some big. I could tell that we weren't going to mesh well in the long run. Thoughts of Tim actually getting to join As Cities Burn didn't seem that far fetched, really. All the guys liked him. Tim and I had been in a couple bands together back home in Arkansas, but the dream was to start our own band and go on tour. Then ACB and Welton happened, and seeing as how we were both opportunistic, there were no hard feelings in going our separate ways. We were both just trying to make it. This run with Welton would be the last time I would tour with Tim.

---

Welton was a pop punk band, but shows are shows and if they could help fill out a tour and share the burden of failure and possibly death (due to it being winter and in the winter it snows up north), then we were all for it. What we learned though is that two unknown bands are in fact not better than one. Instead of just one out of town band on a show filled with locals, the shows had two out of town—and unknown—bands, meaning less room for local support leading to less kids at the shows. Or sometimes...zero kids at the shows.

This unintended consequence of our desire for camaraderie was best illustrated on a snowy evening in Long Branch, NJ, at The Brighton Bar. We were set to play last, an unknown touring band's worst nightmare. It's funny, because eventually you want to headline 'cause that means you are making all the money. Anyways, after Welton finished their set, the few locals that were still there drinking left along with the other bands that had already played. As we took the stage, it came to our attention that the only people left in the bar were Welton, the door guy and the bartender. We were about to play for absolutely nobody. This, had not yet happened to us in our short career. Not one single human that could be legitimately considered a concert attendee. By the end of our set, every one of us was only wearing our underwear or long johns. I think TJ got it started. TJ also worked in some moves that would best be described as "Elainesque." Go look up "The Elaine Dance" Seinfeld episode if you have no idea what I'm talking about.

There is video of this show somewhere. The drummer of Welton, Nic, filmed the whole thing. If only Youtube had been a thing in 2003. Scandal would have plagued As Cities Burn. I can see the headline:

*"CHRISTIAN DEATH METAL BAND EXPOSES THEMSELVES AT ROCK CONCERT"*

As we're winding down our set we though - "What's the point?" -and ended with "The New In Bloom" our heaviest song, and that night, the same song we started our set with. We slowed it down at the end and added some nice deep growls. Felt like a whole new song! Nobody even noticed we had played it twice. Well...there was no one TO notice.

A few days later we would get stuck in a blizzard driving across upstate New York. We had no money for a hotel and so we called in an emergency favor from Colin's sister. She had always said if we were ever in a tough spot to please call and ask for help. This was a tough spot. It was too cold to pull over and sleep in the van, too dangerous to trek on to-wards Cleveland. She even bought a room for Welton. Band hotel party ensued. There was no drinking of tequila or snorting cocaine off the stomachs of local groupies. That's probably what most people think bands do when they get wild. That would all come later in our career...well every-thing except the groupies and cocaine. And usually the "tequila" was actually Southern Comfort, or even crazier, Budweiser.

Actually the craziest thing we ever did back during this time involved Colin's foreskin. One night on this same tour in Virginia Beach, both ACB and Welton were crammed into one hotel room just hanging, and the bass player for Welton - Toby was his name - said he would drink some-one's piss for $20. He needed the money, he declared. Years later he would go to jail for some sexual predator stuff, no joke. Actually, speaking of piss, Colin could do this really cool trick where he would pull his foreskin over the head of his penis and begin to urinate and make his penis look like a blowfish. We called it....The Blowfish. He did this trick this very same night. So in theory there was an opportunity for Toby the sex offender to drink some piss directly out of somebody's exploding foreskin. Anyways, back to the blizzard party.

We decided the best course of action would be to head over to Walmart, buy an inner tube and a rope, then proceed to tie this inner tube to the back of one of our vans and take advantage of the ice and snow covering the hotel parking lot. This lasted about three and half minutes before the desk clerk decided to kill our joy. Fortunately we were able to discover the massive hill on the backside of the hotel that was just perfect for building snow ramps and risking injury. There is video of that somewhere, too. Are you reading this, Nic from Welton?

This is the stuff I remember from early touring days. Because, like I said, the road is pretty boring most of the time. I could hardly tell you anything about the other shows on this tour. It took us stripping down to our underwear and playing for nobody to even have a memorable show experience to share with you. For this, I apologize, but it's the truth. This part of a band's career is completely absent of any glamour or excess. The phrase "nothing to write home about" could not be more appropriate for 99% of these tour experiences. However, we were doing it. We were in the process—a slow one for sure—but we were in the process of achieving what most thought to be impossible. We were SURVIVING. And even with all the shit shows, and no shows, and no shirts or pants while playing the shows, we were having a damn good time doing it.

I didn't miss college one bit. No feelings of regret. Regret comes twelve years later when you sit down to write a book with an empty bank account and realize - "Shit, I should have stayed in college." No, no. There was only pride. The idea of having to be in a classroom or tearing tickets at a movie theater had officially become a thing of the not-so-distant past. From the time I had joined in May of 2003 until the end of the East Coast leg of our tour in January 2004, we had played around 100 shows, all on our own with no support from a label, agent, or manager. Quietly making our own way, hoping for somebody to take notice. We thought our first break would come when we headed west in February. I'm realizing every time I sit down to write this book, we thought a lot of things about the future. We were, as it turns out, pretty much always wrong.

# | 4 |
# Injuries

**People get hurt on the road.** It's the result of having too much time on your hands leading to way too much energy to get out on the stage, partying after a show, or in an ill-advised attempt at athletic competition. Football, pick-up baseball games, made-up parking lot games—pretty much every injury I have witnessed on the road was completely avoidable if only common sense had won out. One of these incidents will go outside the scope of my proposed timeline. But as you will find in these chapters that I think of as "intermissions" from the story, some memories are just too good to pass up.

**Guitars to the Face**

There isn't just one instance of this that sticks out in my mind. The reason being is that it happened so often. I don't remember when Cody, Colin and Pascal finally realized how dangerous the guitar throws around their shoulders and neck were, but it didn't come soon enough. Countless shows involved blood pouring down the faces of my band mates due to being struck by the head of a guitar. TJ once had to receive stitches immediately after the show when jumping off my bass drum, Cody having perfectly timed his guitar throw to land a blow smack between his eyes.

With this and Colin falling off the stage constantly because he was head-banging too hard and losing all bearings on his location, As Cities Burn shows were quite dangerous to play for the first little while I was in the band. Thankfully we decided to just start playing our songs better, sacrificing some trips to the emergency room consequently.

**Bloody Knuckles**

I think this is just my being shitty at drums, but my snare drum head and jeans were covered in blood after every show. I couldn't keep the knuckles on my left hand from smacking my hi-hat every time I would go to hit the snare. This was very painful and downright annoying. But not as bad as accidentally hitting myself in the face, or even worse...penis. Yep. That happens.

**Stabbing Your Brother**

We were in Cleveland Heights, OH, I believe outside of a venue called The Grog Shop. We were opening a tour for Emery, and everyone on the tour was doing some drinking at the venue after the show. I remember it being a really fun night. Then word got around that Toby, the singer for Emery, was on the way to the emergency room with Gary, his brother and Emery's guitar tech, because Toby had in fact stabbed his brother in the hand. Toby in his infinite wisdom was playing with a John Wayne souvenir pocketknife with a 12-inch blade. Toby had just received this knife as a gift from Travie McCoy of Gym Class Heroes, the main support on the tour. Toby was waving the knife around at everyone when his brother Gary threw up his hand to try and get him to knock it off. Toby inadvertently stabbed Gary's hand in between thumb and index finger. Actually it wasn't a stab. It was a gash.

Matt Carter, Emery guitarist, when recounting this story to me used the phrase "gashed a vagina" in reference to the cut on Gary's hand. I guess he remembers the cut looking like the size or shape of a vagina. His words, not mine people. Off to the hospital they went. The doctor told Gary that he came close to losing control of his thumb forever. Toby stabbed his brother. I guess it was a slice. Either way, what a dumbass.

**Breaking Glass on the Boardwalk**

I believe it was summer of 2005 in Virginia Beach, VA. I really loved playing this town. Always had a great party vibe to it. Like everyone was just down to have a good time, especially during the summer. Well the singer for a band called Spitfire wanted to party extra hard that night, I guess. They were also one of those go nuts on stage bands, always trying to one up each other and do the craziest thing they could think of. The stage was backed up to the front of the venue with a window view out onto the street. Cody was standing on the sidewalk watching the show through that window.

The singer saw Cody and started motioning for him to get closer and closer to the window. Once Cody's face was basically touching the window, the singer punched the window. He was trying to be funny and startle Cody. Problem was he punched right through the window and hit Cody in the face. Which means a bunch of glass hit Cody in the face. Cody was sent off in an ambulance, in fear of him having a concussion. Also, lots of stitches were required to keep his face intact. For Spitfire, the show did not go on. It sure was nice of Solid State Records to pick up that hospital bill for Cody; may have saved that singer from a lawsuit. I hope he sent a fruit basket to Brandon Ebel (owner of Tooth and Nail/Solid State Records).

**Swallowed Gasoline**

We took an RV out on the road once because we wanted to camp at Cornerstone Festival in Illinois. It was our first year playing the festival and we thought it would be fun to stay on site, so I hit up my buddy Matt from Arkansas, who had access to an RV. To get home we booked a short run with our buddies in Fletcher (now? Colour Revolt). By that time we had been a touring band for about a year, so the shows were actually decent. The last show of the tour was to be played in

Shreveport, LA. Apparently two or three hundred kids were expected to show up. Very exciting! But then Fletcher runs out of gas between Jackson, MS, and Monroe, LA, on I-20. So we pull over to see if we can be of any assistance. Somebody throws out the idea of siphoning gas out of our RV to give to Fletcher.

Before anybody can even blink Pascal gets on his knees with the tube we planned to use and just goes for it. After a few seconds he flips out and starts gagging and choking and screaming. Dude sucked. You're supposed to blow into the tube when you siphon gas. He seemed so confident that he knew exactly what to do. Now he's laying on the ground like he's dying and, no joke, when Colin comes onto the RV to inform Cody, TJ and myself about exactly what happened, there was laughter. I sat on that RV with a shit-eating grin on my face the whole time.

I don't know if I should feel bad about that, but it happened. That's the truth. Pascal insisted we call an ambulance. Ridiculous, right? He was admitted to the hospital nearby and our show was cancelled. I must be a total asshole, but I'm still mad about that event. Sure it must have been terrible but he was totally fine and by no means did he need an ambulance. Pascal was also a bit dramatic and sensitive in general so I guess it makes sense. But nobody asked him to suck down a pint of gasoline. He wanted the band to pay his ambulance bill. We did not. Are you noticing a common theme with these stories? Dumbass dudes. All of them.

**The Femur**

This one didn't occur until summer of 2010. I was tour managing for Emery at the time and the day of "The Femur" came while passing through Omaha, NE. We had some time to kill before load in, and we had been planning for days to get a real baseball game together with the other bands on the tour. We pulled together enough gloves and some catcher's gear, found a local field that nobody was using and suited up to enjoy America's pastime and my favorite sport. The field was actually more like a sandlot, not well kept, the dirt on the infield almost rock hard.

I am very competitive, especially when it comes to baseball. I played growing up all the way into high school. I'll just say it...I was a damn good ballplayer. I went the way of music instead, a decision I sometimes regret. So when I get a chance to show off my skills, you know I'm going all out. Problem was that I was 27, hadn't played organized ball in ten years, and would drink at least a six-pack of Budweiser a day on tour. I was way out of shape to give max effort on a rough infield.

Being the manager of my team that day, I put myself at shortstop after I pitched a couple innings. Toby, singer of Emery, was playing third base, and I remember Devin, singer and bassist, was out in right field. I remember I made a joke to Devin about whether Emery had health insurance coverage for their crew. He replied with a fatherly-like warning for nobody to get hurt. Josh, keyboard player for Emery, was pitching. I can't remember for the life of me who in the hell was batting, because what would happen on the next pitch pretty much erased most recollection of anything prior to it, other than the details I have disclosed thus far.

The ball was hit to my backhand side on the ground. I started moving to make the play, a play I've made many times before, and I could tell it was going to be a tough one to get to in my current physical form. I should have made a diving attempt. I might have scraped up my knees and elbows, but that would have been better than what actually happened. I lunged, in the way you would do lunges as an exercise, but at full speed.

*CRACK!!!*

It sounded like a tree split in half. I screamed and immediately fell to the ground.

"I broke my fucking leg!!! My leg is broke! It's fucking broke! Oh my God!"

Toby's face was sick, absolutely mortified at the sound and visual of me collapsing to the dirt. I'm laying there breathing frantically, just screaming in agony. It was scary shit, man. After a minute I started trying to convince myself that maybe it wasn't a break. Maybe I dislocated something? Tore my ACL? I couldn't have actually broken my femur RUNNING. Toby was on the phone with his wife, pacing, asking for advice. Later he would tell me he was just telling her that for sure my leg was broken, and how horrifying the sound of the break was. Devin, also on the phone with his wife, a nurse practitioner, was trying to figure out what we should do.

I probably laid on the field for at least 30 minutes, waiting to see if I could try and get up and walk it off. I was in denial. I wouldn't let them call an ambulance, because I didn't have health insurance and I just figured it couldn't be that bad. Finally we decided I had to go to the hospital. Some of the guys went and retrieved the piece of plywood we used as a craps table on the Emery bus casino. The plan was to use it as a stretcher and load me in the back of another band's van. During this time people started praying for me, which is nice and all, but all I could think was, "Quit your praying and get me in that fucking van."

Six or so guys would try and pick me up and move me onto the plywood, with like three of them alone assigned to my leg. As they proceeded to attempt and lift me, I immediately lit up with expletives and screaming to put me down. One really nice Canadian guy had my foot and was trying to be so gentle putting it down, but he was the last one still holding onto me. I specifically remember looking him dead in the eyes and cursing him out. "Let go of my fucking foot right now right now right now right now!" I felt so bad after the fact. He was just trying to help.

The guys retrieved some lids to merch bins and slid them underneath me as well as a pillow under the presumed broken leg. They slid me onto the "stretcher" quite impressively actually. Turns out this is how real medical professionals transfer injured patients. So, great job guys! Now into the van we go. Toby would ride along in the back, with a guy named Jake Ryan driving. I had known Jake for a while from back when he was the drummer for The Chariot, a band As Cities Burn played with a lot. His new band offered up their van as an ambulance.

The hospital was only about three miles away, but it took us 45 minutes to make the trip. Because every little bump or turn would send me into a tirade of cursing and pleading Jake Ryan to slow down. Even when he was down to 5 mph I was still demanding he slow down. The pain of riding in that van was worse than when the break happened. Toby, still terrified by what he was witnessing, chose this moment to reveal to me what the Lord had laid on his heart. In this moment of absolute pain and agony, the culmination of a miserable season of life that saw my band and my marriage crash and burn, Toby declared (in his ultra southern accent, by the way), "Aaron, I know you may not want to hear this right now, but I truly believe this is the best possible thing that could happen to you right now." Who knows what I said to him after that. I probably just kept cursing and screaming. But I know what I was thinking, "Are you fucking kidding me dude?!"

Upon arrival at the hospital, a nurse came out and I guess she was skeptical of the extent of my injury. She brought a wheel chair to the back of the van—yes, a wheel chair—and insisted that I needed to "use my good leg to pull myself out of the van and into the chair". WTF? Visibly annoyed when I told her that was not possible, she went in to get two security guards. Their plan was to pick me up and put me in the wheelchair. I tried to explain we had already tried to have me lifted up onto the plywood, and that it hurt too bad. Still, they tried. And again I cursed them. "Put me the fuck down right now. Stop, stop, stop, stop."

Nurse: "If you dislocated something we have to get you in for an X-ray ASAP son, ok?"

Me: "I can't get in that wheel chair. No way. You have to put me on a stretcher. My leg is broken I think, not dislocated."

Nurse: "We can't X-ray you on that plywood, son."

Me: "Just use it to pick me up and lay it on top of a stretcher and then figure it out!"

Once again annoyed, she goes inside to get the stretcher and they finally lift me up while still on the plywood and roll me inside. I get some pain meds fairly quick, but it's some weak ass shit. They still think I am being ridiculous and that there is no way a 27-year old broke his femur while running on a baseball field. Finally the X-rays come back and a very nice, British orthopedic surgeon arrives to inform me that my femur is in fact broken. He explains that surgery will be needed. A titanium rod will be inserted into my leg and screwed in at the hip and knee.

The doctors must then set my leg. The way I landed on the ground left me in kind of an "Indian style" position with the foot of the broken leg up near the thigh of my other healthy leg. I insisted that they did not need to set it. They disagreed.

This was the worst of the pain and the peak of Toby's terror as he was in the room as they pulled my foot out straight and then rotated my leg around so that my kneecap would point straight up. I feel bad for everyone I came in contact that day that was trying to help me. The expletives and screaming would once again rain down with the wrath and might of a Category 5 hurricane, despite the fact that I was being administered morphine. One doctor asked me my pain level on scale of one to ten. My lips quivering, on the verge of tears, and answered, "Seven?" Toby said the doctor right next to him was whispering in frustration, "Ten, just say ten, man!"

The surgery was successful and Emery went on to the next city without me as I waited for my mom to come to the rescue and take me back to Arkansas to recover. This was the lowest of the low for me. Crippled, recently divorced, unemployed and a $30,000 medical bill. Should have gotten that ambulance, I guess. I definitely needed it way more than the gasoline guzzling doofus.

# | 5 |
# Left Coast Dreams

**"If the show went from five bands** to four bands last minute, why wouldn't they let us play?" we thought. Here we were again with that optimistic thinking, always with the "thinking."

It's February of 2004 and we found out that the Tooth and Nail Tour would be in San Diego the same day as we were coming through. Although we were booked to play The Che Cafe on the UCSD campus in La Jolla, we figured let's swing by the show that people will actually be attending and just see if there is a chance we could jump on. Further Seems Forever was originally supposed to be headlining, but after their singer quit unexpectedly, they dropped off the tour and now Anberlin was top of the bill followed by mewithoutYou, Watashi Wa and our future good friends in Emery.

We plan to just go to the venue, ask if we can play on the floor, and then impress everybody with our insane live show and music that was better than all these scheduled bands anyway! Much respect would be bestowed upon us, and then surely we would be invited to finish out the tour as the opener, since we did WANT to be on Tooth and Nail Records, and we WERE on our way to Seattle to play for one of their A&R guys. That was the whole point of heading west—to get somebody from The Nail out to our show in Seattle. Opening for the Tooth and Nail Tour would guarantee this.

As we arrive at the Epicenter in El Cajon we notice the guys in Emery out in the parking lot organizing some merch. February is quite wonderful in California so everyone is just chilling in shorts and a hoodie. We pile out of our van and head their direction. Hoping they will strike up a conversation with us we kind of creep up on them and just stand there. Their guitar player, Matt, did not seem interested in knowing much about what we were doing. He probably figured we were weird fans. Years later, when I would get to know Matt pretty well, I would learn quickly that Matt hates small talk. I know everyone hates small talk, but he barely even engages in it whatsoever. He will just directly ignore you and make obvious his lack of interest in your existence if you attempt to small talk him. So the next words out of my mouth must have been detrimental to any hopes of making a valuable connection with Emery.

"So...this is the Tooth and Nail Tour, huh?" I asked.

"....Yep." he replied without even looking up from his task at hand.

That was pretty much it. I blew it with the dumbest

question. We had been out of the van for 30 seconds, and already we were annoying people on the tour. We made our way inside to talk to the promoter who immediately directed us toward the tour manager. We asked and he said no. Quickly. Dismissively. Of course we couldn't play. Not even on the floor when doors open. OF COURSE NOT.

Looking back, he did exactly what I would have done when I was tour managing. Bands can't just show up and ask to open real tours with known bands on a whim. Bands don't want the show to be any longer than it is. The truth of the matter is that the show, you know the whole reason you are in a different city every day, is the biggest inconvenience to your day. And anything or anybody that might make your show last longer, is your worst enemy.

But there we were, thinking, "If you would just listen to us! It would help us out so much! We will only play for ten minutes!!" So naive. We lingered for quite a while. I bugged the promoter about it a few more times as I sat around awkwardly watching the bands set up their gear and sound check. Admitting defeat, we headed over to The Che Cafe to hang with the UCSD kids. For dinner, tofu burritos were served. The tortillas were whole wheat. Damn hippies.

Visiting California for the first time is quite thrilling. I had always heard that shows in California were really awesome. There's always tons of kids at the shows and because of all the huge markets in the state, you could easily play shows for almost two weeks. Of course the scenery is beautiful, and things are happening so fast all around you. It really makes you feel like shit is happening for your band. Just being there, all the way from Louisiana, was something for us to be proud of. Our shows weren't great though. Same as in the Northeast, nobody knew us so of course nobody was showing up. We were barely scraping by.

A few days after that San Diego tofu show, we found ourselves in Paso Robles, which is about halfway between LA and San Francisco. This guy Tim (not my friend Tim, a new acquaintance we will call California Tim) was putting on a show for us at the gazebo in the downtown area. Paso Robles was a nice little town, and California Tim was able to get quite a few kids out to the show. What he was able to pay us was enough to save the tour up to that point, and he invited us to stay at his parent's house that night.

The house was basically a mansion, with a theater room, a separate bedroom for everyone and one of those showers that shoots water out from all sides. We all stayed up late talking about music, movies and life in California. TJ made spaghetti and we lived and dined as kings that night. Nights like these are crucial on a tough tour like we were on. Some good will from a promoter and getting to stay with rich people goes a long way in the morale department. The view I woke up to the next morning sealed the deal on my love for California. With rolling hills for miles and miles, my eyes had never been exposed to such a breathtaking landscape and I couldn't believe people actually got to live there. I was hooked.

As previously mentioned, the main goal of this tour was to get somebody from Tooth and Nail Records to come out to our show in Seattle. We felt that they were the ideal label for us, and their bands in our genre were really taking off at the time. Norma Jean, Beloved, Emery, Haste the Day, and of course Underoath. We had opened for a few of their bands on random shows around the south. Haste the Day was exceptionally friendly to us, and their singer, Jimmy Ryan, seemed to really like our band. He told us that he would try and get their A&R guy, Zaine Tarpo, to come out and watch our set if we made it up to Seattle. Jimmy had made sure to get Zaine to dig our press kit out of the pile, and supposedly he was committed to making it out to the show.

———————

After making our way out of California (by way of South Lake Tahoe where we would be caught in a massive blizzard and be forced to spend the night in our van), we headed north full of hope and excitement to have a chance to play for a label we all grew up on. It's hard to describe the impact of Tooth and Nail/Solid State Records if you aren't familiar with them in the first place. I can say this though my first tattoo a couple years down the road would be the album artwork for Craig's Brother's "Lost at Sea" (a band hardly anybody has heard of unless you know that one of their members went on to start Yellowcard). That's how much I loved this label and the bands they put out. Got that shit inked into my arm for eternity.

Zaine Tarpo was a no call, no show. We never found out why he didn't come, or if he had any real intention of coming to the show to begin with. We played our set and that was it. We knew that the time had come for a change in strategy. Our demo and press kit had been out there to labels and agents for over six months, and the result was the same. Zero interest. The West Coast Tour was basically a bust in our minds. Back to the drawing board.

When we returned home to Louisiana we finalized the details to record a new demo. We were almost finished with three new songs: Love At Our Throats, 1:27, and The Nothing That Kills. Tim Jordan invited us to his practice space in Camden, AR, to finish writing and to stay at his lake house. Tim's dad was very wealthy and had all sorts of properties around this small town in south Arkansas, kind of on the edge of The Delta. The sign when driving into town read, "Welcome to Camden...Where History Lives!" Johnny Cash was from a few towns over, but the only thing that was history in Camden was the economy. These were poor folks, except for Tim's dad. Tim was very excited about these new songs. Which was nice, but Tim was excited about everything we did. Still, we weren't holding our breath that this new batch would put us over the top.

We went from Camden over to Cleveland, TN, to record the new songs with Tyler Orr at First Street Studios. This was the beginning of a long working relationship with Tyler and a strange connection to Cleveland. Cody would end up living there for quite some time while recording As Cities Burn's third and final record in 2008. Both my sisters as well as my parents back in the 70s attended Cleveland's Lee University. It's the type of town that sucks people in whether they want to be part of it or not. I was the black sheep of the family, going to a school in Arkansas that was across the street from the school the other guys in my pop punk band, Altar Ego, went to. Then I dropped out of college first chance I had to go piss away my potential in a hardcore band. I'm assuming this is how people viewed it. Obviously that wasn't what I felt at the time. My sisters, probably much wiser than I, followed family suit and enrolled at Lee. And now, here I was in Cleveland, TN, trying to get my band to the next level. Oh, the irony.

The work we did with Tyler for our new demo was crucial to the next phase of our career. Barry Poynter mixed the record in his garage studio in Little Rock. Barry had done some big records for Tooth and Nail/Solid State, most notably Juliana Theory's "Emotion is Dead" and we figured that maybe he would have the ear of the label if it turned out he liked our demo and wanted to send it off for us. He didn't, as far as I know. We were very happy with how the demo turned out. It had been so long since anything new was recorded and the creative process rejuvenated our excitement for possibilities of the future. Once again we put together our press kit with the new demo, updated tour history and a picture on the front cover of us dressed up like the guys from *Boondock Saints* blowing TJ's brains out. Gotta grab their attention, ya know?

We were in the middle of our East Coast April run, planning on heading back west for one more shot at getting Tooth and Nail out to see us, when we met a guy in Nashville who would have a great influence on our journey. His name was Ryan Rado. This guy was, and still is, very popular for many reasons. Yeah he's nice and outgoing and all that bullshit. But the reason you will never forget him is likely because the first time you met him he tried to grab your balls, or tits, or whatever it is you may have. Tourette syndrome can have that effect, after all. He owned it though. It wasn't something he got made fun of for. Everyone loved him and just went along with the insanity. Even the girls. He was always grabbing and kissing and taking your cell phone, tossing it in the air. Oh and riding in a car, Good Lord. Constant braking, unable to resist the urge to swerve into cars parked on the side of the street, and bursts of loud music were expected as he uncontrollably cranked the volume knob on the radio. It was quite the ride.

More importantly, though, Ryan loved As Cities Burn. After our show, I believe it was our friend Russ Hickman that introduced us and Ryan just went on a rant, encouraging us and saying how much he wanted to be a part of it. He explained that he had connections in the industry and that he would really like to try and help. The dude had passion, and at that point, passion was the key ingredient for As Cities Burn. We needed someone in our corner, somebody to really bug the shit out of the people who make decisions. So we told him, show us what you got.

Ryan would accompany us on tour as we did our West Coast run. He was able to convince two key industry guys to attend our show. One was Chad Johnson, who ran Solid State Records. We were very familiar with Chad and his work. His previous label, Takehold Records, had been bought by Tooth and Nail a few years before and now he was playing a big role in the future of The Nail. From now on I will often refer to Tooth and Nail/Solid State as "The Nail".

It's an industry insider term. You know, for industry insiders like myself.

Anyways, Chad's discoveries were amazing, if not downright lucky. Underoath, mewithoutYou, Twothirtyeight, Further Seems Forever, Hopesfall and on and on. He once told me that he had the chance to sign Dashboard Confessional to Takehold, but passed. Not so lucky on that one.

The other guy Rado had set us up to play for, Rory Felton, was the co-owner of The Militia Group. They didn't have any bands as heavy as we were, but their roster and history was strong up to that point with Copeland, Acceptance, Rufio, Noise Ratchet, and The Beautiful Mistake all finding success with the label. We thought it was super cool that he was coming out because we liked all those bands, probably a lot more than any of the Tooth and Nail/Solid State roster at that time.

Rory came and he saw. He didn't say much. I don't even remember if he introduced himself at the show. I saw him and Rado watching the show together, and then I think Rory left as we were packing up. Hardly anyone had attended the show and I figured Rory wasn't too impressed. Rado told us as we loaded the van that Rory offered for us to come stay with him at his place in Long Beach. Always grateful for a place to crash, we accepted the offer. We did not expect what happened next.

Rory sat us down in his living room in a very serious manner. Looking back now, he was kind of a strange guy. Real young, too. Though he was maybe the same age as us at the time. But as he was very successful thus far, we were of course very interested in what he had to say.

"You're going to go to Seattle, and Chad is going to come watch you play, and Tooth and Nail is going to want to sign you. They will make you an offer right away..." - Rory predicted.

We were blindsided. I felt giddy, confused, anxious and hopeful all at once. As we sat in silence, giving him our undivided attention he continued...

"Don't sign anything. You can't sign anything whatsoever. They are going to offer you a shitty deal and then you need to find a lawyer to negotiate."

Rory had already told Ryan all this at the show, so kudos to Ryan for not getting too excited and blowing the surprise music industry coaching session. The next day Rory took us down the street towards the beach for breakfast burritos and then invited us to stop by the label's office. I had no idea at the time that he badly wanted to sign As Cities Burn, but he was never able to convince his partner, Chad Pearson, who had previously worked as A&R at Tooth and Nail. Rory sent us on our way, stocked with confidence and much needed validation.

It didn't even matter that the next five shows that California Tim had booked for us were actually never booked to begin with. We showed up to a closed venue in LA and California Tim wouldn't answer the phone. Never heard from him again.

Since we had no more shows to play in California because the dude turned out to be a flake, we drove all the way to Portland to stay with friends, hike waterfalls, and prepare for our big "showcase" in Seattle, where according to Rory, we would receive a shitty offer for a record deal with our dream label.

Once again, Rado delivered and Chad Johnson did in fact come to our show in Seattle. Unfortunately, we played like total shit, because I played like total shit. It was painful. Dropping sticks, losing the beat, coming into big loud parts too early out of a quiet bridge—what a horrible time for me to forget how to play drums. I couldn't tell if everyone was pissed or just disappointed.

Chad was friendly after the show and even took us to Subway and bought everyone sandwiches. He didn't say much about the show, and he certainly didn't indicate that an offer was on the way. I was devastated. I thought I had ruined our chance at ever getting signed. It was over, and I was probably going to be fired when we got back home. I don't remember who we were staying with that night, but we all went to bed quietly and deflated. Very early the next morning, around 8 or 9 a.m., we woke to Rado's cell phone ringing. He answered, still half asleep, and then his voice perked up.

"Oh hey Chad, what's going on? Ok...ok...ok," excitement building in Rado's tone. "Ok...Ok! Alright Chad we'll see you soon...yeah, thanks a lot Chad."

Everyone is sitting up, still shirtless (well I guess not Cody and TJ as they would sleep fully clothed in jeans) and virtually asleep, waiting with anticipation for Rado to disclose the content of the phone conversation. What seemed like an eternity from the time he hung up to the time words started to come out of his mouth was in reality a millisecond.

"That was Chad Johnson, Tooth and Nail wants to make us an offer."

Dog pile madness ensued. Needless to say we did not go back to sleep.

Less than a year before this day, I had left everyone I knew and loved to pursue something that probably nobody in my life other than Tim believed was worthwhile. On that day I was vindicated. I made lots of phone calls that morning, starting with our biggest fan, Tim. This was the most exciting day of my life to that point. My favorite label, with all my favorite bands from high school, wanted to sign MY band. So cool. We went to the Tooth and Nail office, got our offer and followed Rory's advice, his powwow with us in Long Beach seeming all the more impressive now seeing as how he basically predicted the future. Oh and yes, the offer from The Nail was real shitty. Smart kid. The touring had worked. We were a better band now. Even though I played terrible and ruined our set, Chad was able to see something he liked, and reported back to the boss to sign us now. Ideally, he saw we were the perfect fit for Tooth and Nail/Solid State Records. Our songs were getting better and we were ready to be a real band on a label. This was finally happening. Now we would just have to wait about nine months for the lawyers to sort out all of their bullshit, a wonderful introduction to the shit show that is the music industry.

# | 6 |

# Music Business

**I've incorrectly named this chapter.** A more appropriate name would be, "Clown Show." Look, I don't know much about any other industries or work places. I've done some professional cooking and a couple other random gigs throughout the years, but mostly I've attempted to stay involved in music. Maybe in other industries there is a high percentage of necessary personnel. Maybe there are tons of people that really deserve their job and have a clue. I'm thinking Silicon Valley, or Hollywood, where everyone is just crushing it. I have no idea what the badass to clown ratio is in other industries (let's go ahead and call that BA/C), but in the music industry it breaks down like this:

Justifiably Employed = 7%

Badass = 2%

Clowns = 91%

Whoa baby! As you can see from my sophisticated mathematics above, which was carefully calculated after more than a decade of research and sampling, the music industry is made up of 91% CLOWNS.

Did you think this chapter was going to be a narrative on record deals and publishing, and how to choose a manager or some bullshit? Were you expecting me to walk you through the ins and outs of the bizzzz? I'm sorry to disappoint. There is a great book you can go check out called *All You Need to Know about the Music Business* by Donald Passman. That book tells you all you need to know about...yeah you get it. It's an extremely valuable book if you want to learn about that stuff. Basically you pay $30 for what all the dumb fucks that go to Belmont or USC or Full Sail and major in Music Business pay $80,000 for. Oh wait, they get hooked up with internships so it's totally worth it. No DUMBASS. Buy the book, learn that shit, start a band or go work for a band, go on tour, and by the time all those kids are done with their four-year university degree in CLOWN SHOW, you might have a record deal and already be making shit tons of money (or tour managing a band like that) in which case you automatically trump their degree with credentials and experience. That's what I did anyways. Too bad I just wasn't any good at navigating the bizzz from there.

I always thought, even before we started touring, that I wanted to work on the business side. After all, I had done our booking, and Colin and I were essentially the business side of the band. Colin was basically all business and no art. He had the personality for it. People liked him. I really liked the business stuff, but in a behind-the-scenes way. I was smart and I could learn and apply concepts easily. I was one of those kids that always tested well. But my personality was rubbish, and I could barely make eye contact with people when I talked to them.

Amazingly, I found my way into the bizzz and Colin got the hell out. I always suspected he might be smarter than me. Anyway, by way of tour managing after As Cities Burn disbanded in 2009, I eventually found myself managing Emery in 2013 and a few other bands. It was what I always wanted to do. At the same time I attempted to start a booking agency, and I had already done some studio/producer management. Every one of these endeavors was a crash and burn. Turns out, I was a clown as well. I would quit all that shit near the end of 2013.

But at least I knew I was a clown. I don't know if I've ever really talked to Emery about this, but one of the biggest contributing factors, other than the crippling anxiety I was experiencing 24/7 during that time, was that I truly felt that my position in the industry was totally unnecessary. Getting paid to do fake work and act as middleman. It drove me crazy. I hated every fucking email I received from agents, managers, labels, publicists, etc. There were multiple occasions I wanted to reply, "What in the fuck are we all doing? This is pointless and we are all clowns." Eventually I did start replying to less and less things. And you know what? The tours still happened. Records were still released. The bands did not, as we all suspected, collapse on themselves like a dying star (did I steal this from *Seinfeld*? Or from *The Office?*)

The only job on the business side I had that I've ever felt was an honest day's work was that of the tour manager. I really loved TM'ing. There was shit right in front of you that had to be done every day. It was like mowing the grass. You see your work being completed right in front of your eyes. There was nobody else to make it happen. You were running the show. And I was good at it.

"One more song? I DON'T THINK SO LOWLY PATHETIC OPENER! Please tell me more about how you plan to fit your epic seven-minute set closer into the three minutes that remains in your allotted time to play."

"Oh, you wanna set up a table to spread the word about your non-profit and sell T-shirts? HELL NO. Should have gone through the proper channels ahead of time, newbie."

Gettin' shit done on the reg. But, you gotta be gone constantly to make any money.[5]

Now of course there are some major badass players that make shit move. Big time booking agents, managers that hustle and have a clue, and all these guys that had the vision to start labels and take risks. I really have a lot of respect for those that are doing it right. As long as they aren't total fucking douchebags. Unfortunately, I would have to guess that

---

[5] Tour manager life hack: move to Nashville and get a job TM'ing a country artist. These fuckers have it figured out. They only tour weekends and they put their crew on salary. One TM buddy of mine makes more than my dad and the artist he works for only plays 60-something shows a year. Ninety percent of this chapter does not apply to the country music industry.

the badass percentage would be cut in half if you excluded the douchebags.

I witnessed one of the douchiest and sad acts on Facebook recently. I won't say the name of the guy I am about to lay into, cause let's face it, I'm a pussy and I don't want to burn bridges for the sake of a book that could literally only make me several hundred dollars. If he for some reason ever reads this, he may know I am talking about him. But I also suspect that he has his head so far up his own ass that he would be too obtuse to get the hint. This guy wanted to manage As Cities Burn a long time ago. Obviously we didn't hire him, but years later he built some software that now almost every booking agency on earth uses for data entry and organization, and he broke into the industry big time from there.

I noticed he was posting status updates that were a direct rip off of a popular twitter account. Things like:

"If your LinkedIn work history predates 1990 and you aren't currently in a Porsche near a beach, why would I hire you?"

Or,

"Whenever someone asks how I'm doing, I usually just lie and say 'good', even though I'm doing a lot better than that."

On the twitter account called 'Goldman Sachs Elevator Gossip' (@GSElevator), the owner tweets stuff he overhears at his job. The two quotes above are taken word for word from tweets off that account. This dude was straight up passing off clever tweets about being rich as his OWN on Facebook. How sad is that? The irony is that the GS Elevator twitter account is meant to make fun and expose these assholes. I guess he didn't get the joke. I got sick of it and left a sarcastic comment about how similar his posts were to that twitter account. He deleted all of the posts he had plagiarized and unfriended me.

I have obviously become ultra-jaded as far as the music industry goes. And you would be totally fair to criticize me and just say that I'm jealous of those who are more successful. There is some truth in that for sure. But part of me also wondered if I had to be like the tweet thief to make it. And that was depressing as hell. I couldn't stomach caring about money and status that much. It's probably part of the reason I prefer San Diego so much over LA. Maybe this ranting and complaining wasn't what you expected to read when you saw the title of the chapter. Maybe I'm just feisty tonight because I'm on day 18 of some crazy diet with my wife and I haven't eaten at Cookout or enjoyed a beer in almost three weeks.

But I stand by my assertion that probably 91% of those employed in the music industry could lose their jobs and things would just keep moving right along. Keep the badasses, maybe an assistant here and there, all touring and venue personnel, and we have ourselves a ball game. I could be totally wrong and just butthurt that I haven't found much success in the bizzzz side, but I am so much happier now that I am able to admit that I am in fact, a clown. I don't have it in me to be a badass power player, making shit happen, starting festivals and taking over a corner of the bizzzz. I also don't have it in me to be a douchebag. I just can't fake it. I am proud to say, I am not a douchebag.

I'm just going to stick to playing the drums and now trying to write this book and being happy. But please, if you are thinking about getting into the bizzzz, take my advice and just buy the book and work your ass off for a band or something. If you go to school for this shit, you automatically start off as a clown. And it's hard to work your way out of that when you are $80,000 in debt.

Man, I didn't even touch on the Christian music industry. Talk about a fucked up world. Maybe that's a whole book on it's own. Ok, back to the story now...

# | 7 |

# Long Road To Empire State South

**I guess I haven't yet discussed** the whole Christian aspect of our band. All the members of As Cities Burn during the time period I am covering were Christians, except for Pascal. A good bit of our lyrical content was blatantly in reference to our faith. I don't think it was ever anything intentional, but Cody wrote most of the lyrics and that's what came out. But we never, ever called ourselves a "Christian Band." My contention was there is no such thing. How can a band have a religion? Furthermore, why did a religion need its own genre? Other bands that didn't have Christian members would sing about whatever was going on in their life, or maybe just what they thought about "stuff," but you don't come up with a genre based on lyrical content. It was always very weird to me and felt a little dirty. In the end it's just a way for targeting your product towards a certain group. Identifying something "safe" for church-going kids to listen to.

This was our hesitation with moving forward with Tooth and Nail/Solid State. We didn't want to be trapped in the Christian music industry. Would it affect our touring? Would it affect our reach? Would we feel guilty eventually? Many calculated choices would have to be made to avoid the pitfalls of being labeled a Christian band. A huge one would be avoiding certain Christian festivals at all cost.

In case you are unfamiliar with Christian music festivals, just imagine 30,000 or more youth group kids running around a fairground-type atmosphere being all wacky and shit. Maybe they would dye their hair a crazy color before the festival, or they'd just walk around asking people for hugs. Usually you could identify where they were from, seeing as how their youth minister probably required them to wear a wacky T-shirt with their church name on the back.

The merchandise tent would be littered with vendors selling shirts with slogans such as "I AM SATAN'S WORST NIGHTMARE" or "REPENT OR PERISH." The bands are all pretty much terrible, and the ones that might be good are only there for the abhorrent amounts of money they were offered to play. Come to think of it, the shitty bands were there for that reason, too. It was meant to be completely safe Christian entertainment.

However, there was one exception to this stereotype. Cornerstone Festival. Every summer, out in the middle of nowhere in central Illinois, roughly 25,000 people would gather for the best of "Christian entertainment." It may be hard to convince you that it was cool, a "you had to be there" type of thing. But it was cool. We wouldn't have longed to be a part of it if it wasn't. I talk as much shit about Christians as anyone I know, but it doesn't mean I don't want to be around any of them. I just don't want to be around the doofus Christians. Jesus People USA were the organizers of Cornerstone, and they had created an experience that bands like As Cities Burn and the people we hung out with on a daily basis actually wanted to be a part of. It was much more of a chill hippie meets punk rock vibe compared to the youth group extravaganzas of a typical Christian festival.

Summer of 2004 would be our first Cornerstone experience. When we received the record contract offer from Tooth and Nail, Chad had mentioned he would do what he could to get us a slot to play on Tooth and Nail day. This day of Cornerstone was actually like a primer for the festival. The official first day of Cornerstone was always the day after Tooth and Nail day, which was a good thing because it delayed the arrival of some of the wacky youth group kids. Even though it was a considerably cooler Christian festival than others, it was inevitable that at least some of the goofball youth groups would show up.

     The first bands of the day went on at 10 a.m. with two stages and staggered set times. Seeing as how we weren't actually on the label yet and still virtually unknown, I believe our set started at 10:15 a.m. We were grateful to be there, but figured that time slot would probably be a bust. Quite the opposite. The tent wasn't totally packed like you might see later in the day, but we had a really great crowd come out early to see us. Tons of friendly faces, too. Friends in other bands we had met along the way, people we knew from back home, and some actual fans of the band showed up. This felt like a visible turning point for As Cities Burn. Getting an offer from Tooth and Nail was huge, but from that day forward I noticed that a true fan base was being built.

The great thing about Cornerstone is that you can play multiple times. Ryan Rado had also managed to get us a spot on the New Band Showcase stage, at which we had another great turnout. I suppose we started to build a buzz around the festival and we got asked to play a generator stage. These were impromptu stages set up by festival attendees. You could see a band play in front of 2,000 people one night, and then possibly pass by a generator stage and see 200 kids kicking up dust in a circle pit while the same band played on the grass through a shitty sound system. Our generator show in 2004 was probably as much fun as I ever had playing a show over the course of our entire career. Raw and pure. Reminded me of video I saw of the backyard BMX show when Tim saw ACB play in Baton Rouge. Except here we were thousands of miles from home, with kids we never met who were really stoked to throw down with us. Very cool.

Since we were camping in the RV that year, we spent all of our time on the grounds of the festival. Grilling and chilling. I got some good hangs in with a large group of friends from Arkansas that set up a camp site with a huge Arkansas flag stretched across to alert other festival goers of their Diamond State pride. There was such an amazing feeling of community at Cornerstone that year. It even stripped an asshole like myself of all cynicism and annoyance. I was able to forget about the small—but present—wackiness of Christian teenagers, and just enjoy the moment.

Upon nightfall, the shows became the lifeblood of conversation and reflection. So many amazing artists played well past midnight. I stood on the outside of an overflowing tent and watched Pedro the Lion, amazed at his ability to tame the crowd and engage in actual conversation with the more than 3,000 fans in attendance. Cornerstone Festival will always hold a special place in my heart in the realm of nostalgia. If you keep reading you will have to hear about it twice more, since you know they put it on every year. It was a big deal to bands like us, and worth writing about. Of course our summer tour would come abruptly to an end when the gas-swallowing that you read about a few chapters ago would occur a few days after we left the festival.

———————

We were able to depart from Cornerstone confident that Tooth and Nail/Solid State was the right choice for As Cities Burn. We figured it would only take a few weeks to finalize our record deal. But when your lawyer is also working deals for Snoop Dog and C.S.I. you tend to fall to the bottom of the priority barrel. On the flip side, who knows what strategies the label's lawyer was employing to get the deal he wanted. Maybe after dragging out the process long enough the label was able to get bands to cave in on certain contract details. Our initial offer from the label was for six records, a total shit offer. Our lawyer got it down to three. After that, I have no idea what they negotiated on for the next eight months. Fortunately, this didn't slow us down too much. And we only had half a record written anyways, so there was no rush.

Solid State was putting together a label tour for the fall that would feature new artists only. It was to be called "The Young Bloods Tour." We were offered one of the opening slots even though we still weren't officially signed. The Chariot, a band fronted by Josh Scogin (former vocalist for Solid State band Norma Jean) would headline. He Is Legend, Showbread, and Far Less, all recently signed to Solid State, would round out the bill. For some reason we were asked to take turns playing first with Far Less even though we had way more touring experience than they did as well as a much stronger online presence, which in 2004 meant we had more plays on mp3.com.

 Either way we were excited, because this tour was booked by a real booking agent and As Cities Burn was guaranteed $100 every night. Amazing right?[6] This was significant because we would never have to go back to playing for nothing. Every tour from here on out would be with bands on labels, and mostly booked at actual venues.

 The Young Bloods Tour was pretty damn successful. Kids came out, and I think we pulled our weight and out-

---

[6] *The funny thing about the opener getting $100 to play is that it hasn't changed since 2004, even though gas prices have probably tripled since then. We need Obama to step in and make it right, I think. Opening band minimum wage could be a big issue in 2016.*

drew our $100. There was this kid, Bradley Hathaway, that kind of jumped on the tour as a stowaway. I had seen him perform at Cornerstone, and I guess The Chariot took a liking to him because he was riding with them. He performed spoken word poetry about the hardcore scene and straight edge and how he had never touched boobs. I hated it, and now he was on tour with us, outselling all the bands in merch every night and then complaining about how he wasn't getting paid. I love free market and all that shit, but he wasn't supposed to be on the tour in the first place, had no affiliation with the label, and his presence was affecting the whole tour. It must have been lonely being in his position. Eventually we got used to it and figured the best way to deal was to constantly bust his balls and tear down his cocky as hell exterior.

Ryan Rado had come out on the road with us for this one as well as our buddy who introduced us to him, Russ Hickman. Russ would do merch and Ryan would do Ryan. We didn't need a tour manager at the time, or even a merch guy, but it was fun to have new people along. Russ had been attending Belmont University, studying for a clown degree, and for some reason he was compelled to drop out of college and hit the road with us. Very bold and, in my opinion at that time, admirable. Fuck the system type of shit, ya know? Having Rado out with us was always really fun because the dude is crazy in a good way. New inside jokes would be born on a daily basis as Rado and TJ would be riding up front making up gibberish and coming up with tour catchphrases. I wish I could show you in person the hand signals they concocted for the gas station '"Kum & Go."

Staying with people we would meet was always entertaining with Rado on tour. One night, he noticed that our host had a gun case that was relatively accessible. He informed them that among his many ailments (Tourrettes, OCD, ADHD) that he was a sleep walker and he couldn't guarantee that he wouldn't get up in the middle of the night and blow everyone's brains out. This was news to us. I didn't sleep well that night.

      I don't think Rado liked being on the road very much. He enjoyed the hangs and all that, but the lifestyle was lacking structure and for someone like him, that was a problem. He went home halfway through the tour. Russ ended up embracing life on the road with open arms, and by the end of The Young Bloods Tour he had assumed the role of tour manager. This would lead to a job as tour manager for Underoath shortly after our tour ended. Dropping out of college worked out pretty well for him, I think. Underoath ended up selling ridiculous amounts of records and touring the world. Russ got to go along for the ride and make more money than any member of As Cities Burn ever made.

      The Young Bloods Tour introduced us to tour pranks. I wrote earlier in the book about how the road is pretty boring and there just isn't much to do. A whole lot of hurry up and wait. Once you start throwing five bands on the road together with that much time on their hands they begin to take out their boredom on each  other. Showbread was over the top with pranks. They would do stupid shit like walk up to you while you were eating and yell "FOP!" and then knock your food out of your hand onto the ground. Really sucks to have that happen when you have no idea how you are going to pay for your next meal. Rubbing human feces under the door handles of another band's van wasn't out of the ordinary for those guys. The best we could come up with to get them back was to switch out their stage water with bottles of vinegar. Colin, TJ, and I executed this flawlessly in Wilmington, NC, at The Soapbox.

Showbread had seven members so it was quite satisfying to watch them spit out their vinegar one by one. Being the pranksters that they were, once a band member would take a drink, they wouldn't alert the other guys that their water was in fact vinegar. We got 'em all. Last night of tour they filled our van with BBs. Extremely annoying to listen to those roll around the floor all night on the six-hour drive home from Tallahassee. At least I-10 along the Gulf Coast is very flat.

Something I had to learn very quickly was that As Cities Burn probably wasn't going to tour with a lot of bands I actually liked. I was not a fan of any of The Young Bloods Tour bands, but there we were hanging out every day building shallow tour friendships. Being in a heavy band significantly lowered the chances of me digging the music of our tour mates. I hardly ever watched the shows on that tour. But I'm sure the other bands felt the same way. Deep down, every band thinks theirs is the best on any given tour. No matter how stoked you act about somebody's set or how enthusiastically you gush over their most recent release, narcissism prevails and in the end you will find yourself cruising to the next show, talking shit about everyone on tour and how shitty the bands are. It's nothing personal, just delusional.

We did have one fan from that group of bands: Josh Scogin. He approached us about helping produce our record. The decision had been made during the course of the tour that we would record with Matt Goldman in Atlanta. Matt had produced Copeland and a few other cool indie bands, as well as The Chariot. We had no interest in having a producer who only made heavy records. Since Josh lived in Atlanta he thought it would be cool to get involved, mostly in terms of helping with vocal production. Cody and TJ had been pretty into Norma Jean back when Josh was screaming for them, so the offer was exciting for them. I didn't really know what to make of it, but it seemed nice that somebody else who was further in their career liked our band. It did kind of weird me out that the dude liked to dip his pizza in mayonnaise.

We were scheduled to go into the studio with Goldman in February of 2005. Once The Young Bloods Tour was over we still had to finish three more songs in about a month's time. As Cities Burn did not write quickly. We had started writing the ten songs that would eventually be on our first full length in the summer of 2003. We were well into December of 2004 and only had seven ready to go. Some bands write twice as many songs as they have room for on an album. As Cities Burn never wrote any amount of songs over what was necessary to fill the album. Cody really took his time with song ideas and the content of the songs. Once he would come up with a rough structure for a tune, we would all get together and try and make it a song. Back then "songs" meant we would play a part for a minute, then start another part, then slow down, play another new part, speed up, play another new part, and so on. Having a verse and a chorus that repeated wasn't even on the radar.

Some tension had started building between the band and Pascal around this time. Well, maybe it was more Pascal and I. I can't honestly remember. We were getting together to write almost everyday in Mandeville, LA, on the North Shore of the lake. Pascal lived in Metarie, which was on the South Shore. He kept pulling this shit where he wouldn't show up for practice and when we called to see why he was late, he acted as if he had no idea a practice was scheduled. It pissed me off because from my perspective he would intentionally disconnect himself from the "inner circle" of the band, just so he could accuse us of keeping him out of the loop. When we would actually be writing, Pascal would make lots of suggestions for drum parts, because he was also a drummer. But I genuinely disliked almost every idea he threw out. He was a marching band kid and his style had all sorts of flams, flaps and phalanges (Dave Chappelle show anybody?) scattered throughout. Looking back, I know I kind of sucked at drums at the time, but his ideas were just bad. This was the beginning of a growing conflict that would soon shake things up in As Cities Burn.

We were able to finish the last two songs by the end of January 2005, and I believe those songs turned out to be the best on the record.[7] I think Cody was really worried we weren't going to finish in time. Several times during the tail end of this writing process we would end a run-through of a song and Cody would just sit with his head down and hair draping over his guitar, seemingly ready to admit defeat. After a few seconds he would look up with this grin as if he wanted someone to confirm what he was feeling. The music was shit. As in bad. I don't think it was a lack of confidence on his part. I think he just expected a lot out of himself. His standard for success was higher than most. This is something I would see ring true in many aspects of Cody's life over the years. He wanted shit to be done right. It didn't matter if a million people loved a song and wanted to give him all their money to be able to listen to it. If he wasn't feeling it, he would trash it.

Fortunate for As Cities Burn, we were able to assure him that we had done our best and it was time to go make a record. It had now been nine months since we first played for Chad in Seattle. Our record deal STILL wasn't finalized, but the label was moving forward with sending us into the studio regardless. We loaded up the rig, headed northeast to my birthplace and the home of the greatest baseball team on earth. Somebody was gonna give us $25K to record some music we wrote. Insanity.

---

[7] *Thus From My Lips' and 'Admission: Regret' were the two songs, for all you fans out there who may have been curious...*

# | 8 |
# Money

**Throughout most of this book,** I have communicated with great emphasis how poor dudes in bands are. It wasn't until over a year after I joined the band, that I actually got paid at the end of a tour and then it was only like $80. That is NOT an exaggeration. In the 14 months between May 2003 and July 2004, I made $80. I was ecstatic when we received this humble, but well deserved share of As Cities Burn "profits." Took me about 24 hours to spend it all. Why? Because band dudes are fucking terrible with money.

It doesn't matter what the amount of money, band dudes will always spend just about every penny on stupid shit. Some faster than others, but in the end it will all be gone. Sure I've had some friends who bought houses while they were still touring full time, but a few of them lost those houses when their bands didn't continue to blow up at the rate that they expected. Most of us don't take into consideration that eventually it will all end. The money coming in will decrease drastically, and then you got to figure real life out.

Now I am speaking only in terms of my world. And in my world nobody was getting million dollar publishing deals. Well I guess in Tim's world they were (see: All American Rejects), but that doesn't count for the purposes of this chapter. We are talking about guys I actually toured with or were just generally in our "scene." The biggest band we were friends with, Underoath, made a ton of money. But it's not like they are retired now. They all have jobs. Maybe they have some money in the bank, but in the grand scheme of life it's only a small leg up on the rest of us. It's amazing the misconception that fans have about bands and their money.

I'm sure some fans of Underoath think none of them ever have to work again. Maybe that's not entirely unreasonable if you don't have a grasp on the economics of a band operation and how we generate income, and most importantly how we sustain that income. Underoath did have two gold records. I suppose somebody could naively liken them to that of Alex Rodriguez in terms of wealth.

This concept of unreasonably comparing your favorite band to say a famous athlete is something quite interesting to me. It's best illustrated in an episode of Seinfeld where Jerry and George are in a locker room at their health club and they see Keith Hernandez (first baseman for the 1986 World Champion Mets) walk in. Jerry is thinking about talking to him, an idea that George finds to be absurd. Jerry

Jerry: "Hey, should we say something to him?"

George: "Oh yeah, I'm sure he loves to hear from fans in the locker room."

Jerry: "Well he could say hello to me. I wouldn't mind."

George: "He's Keith Hernandez. You're Jerry Seinfeld."

Jerry: "So?"

George: "What, are you comparing yourself to Keith Hernandez. The guy's a baseball player, Jerry, Baseball!!"

Jerry: "I know what he is. I recognized him. You didn't even notice him."

George: "What...you are making some wisecracks in a night club... wo wo wo. The guy was in game SIX two runs down two outs facing elimination."

"Baseball player, Jerry, baseball!" is a perfect example of why I feel so ridiculous every time somebody tells me that As Cities Burn is their favorite band of all time or acts at all starstruck around a member of a band that I am buddies with. I'm not trying to be mean to the fans or anything, but we are all small time compared to baseball players. Even the members of a big band like Underoath (or another band of similar size) probably only made around $250K a year at their peak. Compare that to a rookie on an MLB team where the minimum salary is $550K a year. So the 23-year old relief pitcher sitting on the bench most of the game who is as green as they come is making double what the biggest bands in my world made.

The gap between me being starstruck if I met Chipper Jones ($150 million or so made in his career, played in front of 30,000 people every night, won an MVP and a World Series championship) and you being starstruck by meeting Cody from As Cities Burn ($50K made over six years and played for 3,000 people a couple times) is significant to say the least, in the economical sense anyways. Excuse me if I feel totally fucking retarded the next time I get asked for an autograph, because it's likely that later that day I am raking the leaves at the house I rent to save $100 on rent next month.

What's REALLY funny is when somebody applies this logic to me specifically. When my wife started working at her airline job three years ago as a customer service agent, she realized there were a few As Cities Burn fans that worked with her. (This is not uncommon in Nashville. I was at a super hipster bar here in East Nashville recently and much to my surprise the super hipster bar back was a fan.) The conversation between my wife and her co-worker went something like this:

Co-worker: "So, what does your husband do?"

Wife: "Well he's a drummer, and he toured with a band for a long time..."

Co-worker: "Oh cool. What was the band?"

Wife: "Well, are you familiar with like Tooth and Nail bands at all?"

Co-worker: "Yeaaahhhh..."

Wife: "Well... he played in a band called As Cities Burn..."

Co-worker: "WHATT?!!! WHY DO YOU WORK??!!"

In this guy's mind, me sending my wife off to work was so utterly insane because the riches I must have accrued during my tenure as the drummer for As Cities Burn surely was enough to ensure our financial security for the remainder of our life on earth. Why in God's name would she need to be working? It's a frustrating reality that this guy couldn't have been more off the mark in his assessment.

The most I ever made playing with As Cities Burn from 2003 to 2009 was about $1,500 a week... when we were TOURING. That kind of income didn't start until a few years into touring after our first record found some success. When we were home it was virtually nothing. There was the occasional publishing royalty check and advances before going in the studio, but for the most part if we weren't on the road, there was no money to be had. I would say in that six-year period that we were a full-time band I maybe took home $50K. That might be an overestimate. That's $50K. For *six* years. That's what the U.S government would refer to as "below the poverty line". Think about that next time you are accusing a band of selling out or only caring about money.

There is a damn good chance they aren't making near as much as you may think.

When we did get money, we mostly spent it at bars, Apple stores and Urban Outfitters. I spent ungodly amounts of my income at Urban Outfitters in between 2006 and 2008. Maybe it's still cool to shop there, I wouldn't know. But for band dudes during that time, it was a mecca. The best days of tour were when you played somewhere like Ybor City in Tampa that had copious amounts of ways to blow your money: Urban Outfitters, movie theaters, sushi. A day off on tour in a place like that could easily see me blow $200. That's a lot when you think about that whole $50K in six years factor.

Don't get me started on gambling. Vegas was a black hole of financial despair for band dudes. On the road, after a show your adrenaline is high. You got 20 other dudes around you ready to go out and go nuts, live like there is no tomorrow. There is nothing in the world that can compare to an entire craps table at a Vegas Casino being at full capacity with tour mates. Everybody is cheering and high fiving, testosterone running high. Other people at the casino are wondering who you are and why you are having so much fun. These were experiences that I truly cherished, despite the financial consequences.

As Cities Burn loved the greyhound races in Florida. Sometimes we would rush to pack up our gear and even our merch and bail on the show early to make it to the track. Cheap beer, cheap bets and fast dogs. Some real white trash Florida shit. Love it. Rolling dice was another popular way to spend/lose money on tour. Green rooms often turn into underground gambling venues. Emery even set up a casino on their bus running craps and a blackjack table. The pots were never too big, but sometimes you could make out with an extra $50 in beer money. Once in New York City, in the bar of the Knitting Factory, TJ and I took a dice game called "Threes" to a jackpot of around $180. TJ had lost like four rounds in a row but kept betting double or nothing. I let it go for one round too long, and we ended up back at zero. Could really use that money now, dammit.

In a nutshell, instead of saving up for a down payment on a house, most band dudes blew their money gambling, buying clothes and gadgets, buying equipment and fancy road cases that were entirely unnecessary (I'm looking at you Colin and Cody...Ok I bought one, too), and sushi. Probably bad sushi at that. Anthony Bourdain would probably be very disappointed in my sushi choices throughout my touring years.

It's probably better that I spent all the money. If I had bought a house, how in the hell would I have paid for it after the band broke up? Remember, I dropped out of college when I was 20 to go make $10K a year! So in a roundabout way, my terribly irresponsible spending habits saved me a whole world of problems. Always looking on the bright side of delusion: a band dude's manifesto for financial security.

# | 9 |
# Making Hits Behind a Pizza Shop

**"Live...I show no mercy on my cymbals."** These were some of the first words out of my mouth to Matt Goldman. As soon as I said it, I knew it was so incredibly retarded (pardon my language to all you quickly-offended, politically-correct guys and gals). Couldn't take it back though. Those words were OUT there. And my band has never forgotten it.

Goldman was trying to talk to me about how he wanted me to hit my cymbals for the sake of the recording. When you are tracking drums you have to let the cymbals move and do their thing. I know that now of course, but back then, just a dumb young kid, Goldman knew I needed coaching.

I wasn't that good at drums going in to make our first record. There was even a point a little less than a year earlier, after we had received our offer from Tooth and Nail, that I thought I was gonna get kicked out of the band. Remember that terrible show I played in Seattle in front of Chad Johnson? Well, I played equally as bad the rest of the tour. Outside a warehouse/ skatepark hardcore show in Wichita, KS, the guys pulled me aside and gave me a pretty brutally honest talking to about my performance. I hate confrontation, and it made me feel really weird for a while. It all got smoothed over, but I still wasn't that good going into recording.

Goldman's studio was shacked up next to Five Points Pizza in Little Five Points, a hipster neighborhood popular with the homeless just east of downtown Atlanta. Very cool place to spend four or five weeks hanging out, if only we had money to blow. We were mostly still on Silly Pack budgets with the occasional splurge at the pizza shop or some Mexican food at El Myr down the street. We got a discount on an extended stay Marriott in midtown due to Pascal's uncle hooking it up. Turns out there wasn't anything to do around there, so most of our days would be spent lurking on Myspace for girlfriends[8] and watching DVD's.

Drums are usually up first in the recording process. Unless you are making a live record or some other sort of cool thing where you spend tons of time in the studio playing around and seeing what sticks. But we were a post-hardcore band trying to make a record in four weeks, so the strategy

---

[8] *TJ actually did find a girlfriend, the only reason he made a Myspace account. About a year and a half later he married her.*

was to take it piece by piece. Drums, then bass, then guitars, then vocals. That's the formula.

We didn't spend a lick of time on pre-production. I remember trying to get Goldman to really dig into the demos with us and analyze the songs, and as we were listening I could tell he wasn't paying too much attention. I say this not to criticize Goldman, but to just laugh at ourselves. The demos at that point were useless. He knew this. There was a process he was going to guide us through and sitting down and listening to our shitty demos that we thought were such a big deal was not part of the process.

As Cities Burn loved to change tempos. I don't know if there was a single song on that record that didn't have a tempo change, sometimes multiple tempo changes. It was out of control. And making a click track, otherwise known as a metronome, to go along with it was a pain in the ass. Even more of a pain in the ass? A drummer who sucks at playing to a click.

It's normal to schedule five or so days to work on drums for a record like we were doing. It takes some time to get tones dialed in, and it's fun to change things around and try different setups. But it shouldn't take a drummer five days to track ten songs that he helped write.

I took all five days and then some. Nowadays I can easily knock out the drums for a full length record in two days or less without even hearing a song before I stepped into the studio. To my credit, on the first day of tracking Goldman's recording software kept crashing his computer and he had to bring in this kid Jeremiah[9] to run ProTools so we could get moving. I did my part in making sure we didn't move too quickly.

Our eventual single on the record, "Bloodsucker Pt. II," gave me the most trouble for some reason. I was all inside my head by the time we got to it, convinced that I wasn't good at drums anymore. Convinced that I hadn't been playing drums for over a decade. Convinced that I had no business playing on this record. I believe it was the last song I tracked for the record. I kept trying and trying to nail it, for hours, maybe. Goldman finally gave his signature "It'll be finnnnneeee," and told me he would work on it that night and to go home.

Work on it meant edit the shit out of it. So embarrassing to admit that, but it's the truth. Came back in the next day and thought, "Wow I'm not that bad!" Paranoia eventually set in and for years I have wondered whether my drums actually got re-tracked by someone else: Goldman *is* one the most badass drummers out there. There are plenty of studio tales involving band members having no idea that what they hear on their record isn't actually them playing. That a producer called in a studio musician to pick up the slack and make it right. I'm 99% sure that didn't happen in this case. But it's always been in the back of my mind. Please God...I hope nobody ever tells me if that WAS the case. What's the difference though? Not like I had any artistic integrity of my own.  I was just trying to rip off Further Seems Forever

---

[9] *Jeremiah ended up being the original drummer of a little band called Manchester Orchestra.*

drums parts as much as I could. If someone else was able to better execute that mission, good for them.

The personal tension that was building between Pascal and myself became noticeable to Goldman when Pascal went to track bass. We were totally out of sync. It's like we hadn't even discussed how the bass and drums would line up to each other. The goal is to have the bass drum and bass guitar locked in with each other. Pascal was nowhere close. It's because we hadn't talked about it. We hadn't even considered it. I was doing my thing. He was doing his thing. And that was that. I'm sure Goldman enjoyed having to figure that out.

Goldman was and is a really great guy. We made two full-length records with him, and years later Cody and I made an EP with him for a different band. He was so gracious and patient with us in all of our infinite naivety about the recording process. We even told him we wanted As Cities Burn to be listed as a Co-Producer. No clue about anything or what that even meant. But Co-Producer's we were.

Goldman never got angry with us, and he wasn't there to force his vision on us. He was very clear that we were making OUR record, not his. We loved that about him. He was very comfortable to be around, and the dude is a conversationalist. There were times where we thought, "Shouldn't we be working instead of talking about The Beatles?" We were there to make a record that was going to change the world! How dare he focus on or think about anything else!

This lackadaisical style that Goldman is notorious

for can be difficult for some bands to adapt to at first, especially if you have never made a real record before.

We came in with the notion that if we aren't grinding it out 12 hours a day, we must not be working hard and how is this ever gonna get done. Goldman was the master at taking that mentality and instead instituting a culture of studio hangs. We enjoyed constant drop-ins from random folks. A guy named Troy Stains was at the studio almost every day. He didn't work there or anything. Just hanging. If he showed up at the right time, Goldman might recruit him to play the lap steel or some other weird instrument. Glow in the Dark Studio often lacked in efficiency and time management, but that place excelled in the area of creativity and hangs.

One day we were all sitting in the control room (squeezed in there like sardines in a can because well, it was really small) and somehow *The Office* came up. We were smack dab in the middle of recording a guitar part or something when Goldman said, "Wait, you haven't seen *The Office*? Oh we gotta watch it!"
Okaaaayyyyyyy....

We spent the next two hours watching David Brent and his crew of dilapidated employees, having to keep the subtitles on because the British accents were so damn thick. We would finish an episode and think, "Ok now back to work, right?" Nope. Anxiety was high in that 14x6 control room. "How are we ever gonna finish this record?" was the thought on everyone's mind. But dammit, *The Office* was funny. I borrowed the DVDs and spent the rest of our time in Atlanta finishing the series. I am probably more grateful towards Goldman for introducing me to the comedic gold of Ricky Gervais than for the fine work he put into making two of our records.

————————

About halfway through the recording we got word from our lawyer that our record deal was being finalized and would soon be ready to sign. It was nerve-wracking starting the recording process without being officially signed to the label. Happy and ready to get it over with, our lawyer sent the contract to us in Atlanta with instructions. We all sat down at a table in our hotel and signed away. It was so damn anti-climatic because it took ten months for that fucker to be negotiated. I always pictured the signing being so ceremonial and exciting. But by that point I was just happy to get it over with. Sucks for this book as well. I just had to throw in the story about actually inking a record deal in the middle of making a record. But as I keep saying, that's how it happened. The truth is just boring sometimes.

Band dynamics did get weird shortly after the signing. Just a couple days later, Pascal sat us down at the hotel and informed us he was leaving to go home and that he needed a break from the band. Something to do with family, but he would never be specific about the reason. He just needed to go. Welp, ok then.

Am I a dick if I say I was pretty stoked? Yes? Ok, but that's the truth. Sorry y'all. I didn't really understand the concept of taking a break from your band. I remember ranting to Colin about how Pascal had quit the band. That was what he did. He QUIT. The idea of holding his spot until he felt compelled to waltz back in was so bizarre to me.

We didn't have a vacation benefits' package that I knew of. What were we supposed to do in the meantime? Fill-ins, I guess. This whole debacle encapsulated so much of why I didn't get along well with Pascal. I can be incredibly insensitive and polarizing. And when people do vague, "woe is me" shit like this, it sets me off. You won't find one of those "Tolerance" or "Co-Exist" stickers on my bumper any time soon.

Funny that after he left such a weight was lifted. The whole time he had been there he had projected this attitude that he was giving up so much and was even kind of put out by having to be away from home. Everything just got more chill from there on out because the rest of us really had a good time together. TJ and Colin had a real good time out on the town one night, and TJ came back to the hotel having lost Colin. An ice storm had begun to hit Atlanta, but TJ went back out looking for him in the van. He found him about three miles down the road into downtown on Peachtree St. near what is now The Westin. When Colin finally got back to the hotel, his hair had turned to icicles and he was exclaiming how he had "walked all the way to Buckhead, mannnn," which was about six miles in the opposite direction of the way he actually went. Funny shit. What an amateur.

Despite the loss of a band member and Colin's drunken excursion to Buckhead, recording was moving along. The day TJ was starting vocals he and I executed a nice little prank on Goldman and the guys. I was in the control room and had the urge for a nice cold Snapple Apple, so I left to fulfill my desire. To get outside the studio you had to walk straight through the tracking room, which at that time was pitch dark because TJ liked to record in the dark. As I was walking through I grabbed him and told him to let me do his screaming part. TJ obliged, with joy. The first song they were tracking for him was called "Admission: Regret." There is a long intro with no vocals and then a big ole screaming part to accompany the band coming in heavy. I lay into it hard, pushing my vocal chords to the very extreme of their limits. And of course, it is awful. TJ is laughing his ass off (quietly, so not to blow our cover), and Goldman stops the track.

"Ok...Let's try that again. Are you ok? Do you need some water?"

TJ flips on the lights to reveal the switcheroo, to which a huge feeling of relief sweeps the control room followed by laughter and acknowledgement of the brilliance of such a joke. I think Goldman thought the whole record was about to go down in flames, bless his heart.

Of course TJ went on to crush it on vocals, with the help of assistant producer Josh Scogin who is kind of a king of sorts when it comes to screaming vocals and making them catchy. Josh did an amazing job helping Cody and TJ see how to get the most out of even one single lyric. For fans of the record, the best example would be the "Regret" over and over on "Admission: Regret". I mentioned before that I was skeptical of having Josh work on the record, as I didn't see the value in having yet another voice and opinion to have to sift through. My skepticism was ill-conceived. He was an invaluable piece to the success of the record.

Even with our breaks to watch British comedy and listen to Goldman and Troy converse about all sorts of nerdy things, we finished the record on time. And I guess, despite my rocky introduction to playing drums on a record that actually matters, we were all pretty happy with it. We had no idea if Goldman liked it. He at least thought parts of it were cool. That was good enough for us.

For those of you who may not know, after you track a record you must have somebody then mix the record. We were of the school of thought that it is always beneficial to have a different person mix. Good to get fresh ears. We sent it off to Mike Watts at Vudu Studio on Long Island, NY. Mike had worked with some pretty cool acts, and that would continue to be the case after we worked with him. Hopesfall, The Pixies, As Tall As Lions, The Dear Hunter and on and on. I'm not sure how we ended up working with him, but he did a tremendous job. I remember getting tons of compliments on the mix and production of our record from our peers. Aaron Gillespie, drummer for Underoath, once gushed to me about the drum sounds declaring how "real" they sounded. No word on what he thought about the actual performance. I can take a guess though.

We did travel to New York to hang out for a good portion of the mix, which was in retrospect mostly pointless. It's one of those things that young bands are insistent about because I suppose we didn't trust anyone to do what we wanted. It's a form of micromanaging—always wanting to look over everyone's shoulder to make sure their work is up to your impossible standards. Mike would basically kick us out of the studio and then let us know when we were allowed to come listen. He was a real tough New York type of guy too, so we didn't argue. With a thick accent he pronounced our band name "Acid-ies-bern," all one word in a very laxed and quiet New York dialect. Dude loved to cuss, too. He was damn good at it. I would say I learned a great deal about cursing from the man.

The whole time we were there we stayed in the studio apartment. We would order badass pizza almost every day, or get subs from a shop not too far away. It was March, so still freezing outside with snow on the ground. Mike kept saying maybe one night we would get a stretch hummer and take it into the city to see a show or something. Never worked out unfortunately, and we were still too poor to go into Manhattan and have any fun. That would change in a few months.

We went back home to Louisiana to wait. Wait on the record to get mastered. Wait for the label to decide when the release date would be. Wait to see what our touring schedule would look like for the rest of the year. Who in the hell was gonna play bass? As we were just sitting around for a couple months, Colin taught me how to kill time in New Orleans.

At this point I was 22 years old and had never had a sip of alcohol in my life. For a while it was because I was the typical youth group kid who thought drinking was of the devil. "I mean I can have a good time drinking some Mountain Dew! Nobody needs alcohol!" I probably said. And sure nobody needs alcohol, but damn is it fun.

One night we went down to the French Quarter to hang with our friends Mel and Leslie, the ones who lived in New York that we stayed with but were now were back home in New Orleans. We were doing the typical French Quarter activities. Walking down Bourbon Street, everyone with a drink in their hand but me. I had been considering it recently, but still had not taken the plunge. Mel couldn't take it anymore and offered to buy me a daiquiri. I accepted.

It was weird at first, and now I know I had just tasted all the cheap alcohol you get in a strawberry daiquiri on Bourbon Street) But then came the numbness. A few blocks down the street I began to declare enthusiastically, "I CAN'T FEEL MY FACE!" Colin, being a veteran party guy from his bro days at LSU enjoyed this very much. It was like seeing a kid discover a candy shop for the first time, except the kid is 22 years old and realized he had been missing out for so long on this candy and now he was overwhelmed with joy. I finished my daiquiri and we headed to Molly's on Decatur, a chill spot on...Decatur St. and I started on the Amaretto Sours, very sophisticated and masculine of me. Fortunately, I stopped before everything got out of control with only a mild hangover the next morning for me. Don't worry, plenty of puking and declarations of regret to come in later chapters.

With many questions to be answered in the waiting game we were playing, there wasn't much else to do other than head to New Orleans a few times a week and watch movies. This was the life of a band off the road. Not home long enough to get a job, but home so long where you start to feel like a deadbeat. Trips to Baton Rouge and random local shows would fill the weekends while fueling our metabolisms with the likes of Raising Canes' chicken fingers. Artery clogging, but oh so good.

Finally our release date was set: June 21, 2005. Preparations would begin for what would be a brutal touring schedule from May straight through to December. Like that kid in the candy store for the first time (and me with disposable income to spend on alcohol for the first time), our eyes were bigger than our stomach. We bit off more than we could chew, and we would pay the price.

# | 10 |
# Fan Festivus

**I've been dreading writing this chapter.** Every time I bring it up to my wife or mention a thought regarding the content of what you are about to read, she rolls her eyes and says, "Oh dear, tread lightly." Not like Walter White says to Hank in that garage...more loving and sweet. But she, more than anyone, has heard the extent and offensiveness of my ranting about fans.

I truly do love the fans that supported As Cities Burn. I really mean that. I am thankful for every T-shirt they bought, every ticket they purchased to one of our shows, every kind word we have received in person or through the 'ole world wide web (trying to get my word count up, so I used world wide web instead of just 'internet'). I genuinely appreciate that connection between band and fan.

Obviously a band is NOTHING without fans. The fans make it possible to create art and maybe pay some bills along the way. I love them. Hell, I love the fans so much I married one. As Cities Burn was one of my wife's favorite bands before we ever met. And since I thought she was damn hot and like the best person I had ever met, I made sure to lock that down ASAP. The trade off for her—since I'm kind of an asshole and not as good looking as her—is that she gets to have sex with the drummer from one of her favorite bands. Good deal, don't you think? It's not an even trade, but...it's something.

So, while my love for fans of the band runs deep, I must quote Frank Costanza to get the ball rolling into shit talking, "I've got a lot of problems with you people!"

We can start light here. Let's easssse into the fan-hating. What's the deal with nobody recognizing me? Here's an example.

Outside of Chain Reaction in Anaheim, As Cities Burn had just finished playing for a sold out crowd. I don't remember who we were opening for, but that doesn't matter. Point is, it was a crazy awesome show with a shit load of crazy awesome fans. I was outside in the parking lot packing up my drums, standing right next to Cody packing up his guitar. We were both soaking wet with sweat from the show. It was quite obvious that we both had just gotten off the stage.

A group of kids walk up and start talking to Cody about the show. Telling him how awesome it was and all that. I face towards them while packing up my drums to be courteous and listen to them gush about how much they loved As Cities Burn. To be clear, there was no mistaking that I was the drummer for As Cities Burn. I was packing up my drums, right next to Cody, who was right next to my MASSIVE purple road case which had AS CITIES BURN spray painted on all sides.

They proceeded to ask Cody to autograph the T-shirts they had purchased. Cody obliged them and continued to engage in small talk about the show. I stood there waiting, figuring they would want me to sign next. After all, I was the drummer of the band they loved so much. I stood, waiting...waiting...waiting. They said "Thanks Cody!" and looked at me as they walked away. I hate signing autographs anyways. What a stupid thing to do. Mess up a perfectly good T-shirt with a sharpie? It's not like Cody is Keith fucking Hernandez. Asshole fans. Obviously totally over this, and not in any way bitter that they either didn't recognize me even though I was standing next to my AS CITIES BURN drum case, packing up drums next to the singer for As Cities Burn. I'll probably forget about this occurrence from ten years ago tomorrow.

Speaking of not getting recognized, a couple years ago I was at an ice cream shop on lower Broadway in Nashville with my wife. As per usual I was wearing a T-shirt of a band I was in. (As stated before in this book, once you hit 30 it just doesn't matter. Wear your own band's T-shirt till the day you die I say.) This wasn't an As Cities Burn shirt though—it was Hawkboy. Hawkboy is a band Cody and I started in 2011. We put out a couple EPs, did a few tours around the country. Good times. It was just him and me. Two people. Meaning I was 50% of the band. If ever my chances of being recognized by a fan were good, this was it. I was ONE HALF of the whole band.

So, there I am in the ice cream shop, wearing the Hawkboy shirt. I get up to the counter and the guy working says to me,
    "AWWWW DUDE!! HAWKBOY. That's a badass shirt man. They are one of my favorite bands. So, what kind of ice cream you want?"
    Hawkboy is one of his favorite bands, and yet the drummer and exactly ONE HALF of the band is standing right in front of his face about to order ice cream and he doesn't have a clue. As one would imagine, my wife laughed her ass off afterwards.    Let's talk about the girl who saw TJ smoking a cigarette at a bar. We were hanging out on a day off in Little Rock, AR, and we went to a show at Juanita's. I'm guessing we had friends playing, because typically the last thing on earth you want to do on a day off of tour is go to another show.
    We were quite popular in Little Rock, so the idea that a fan of ours would be out and recognize our singer was likely enough. But what she saw that night was apparently detrimental to her fandom of As Cities Burn. We received an email later that night that explained how she had seen us at the show and that she saw TJ smoking a cigarette. She went on to tell us how she had struggled and prayed and even cried, trying to figure out how she was going to deal with this let down. How was she going to go on, now that the singer of her favorite band was publicly using a tobacco product? The only option was to denounce her fandom and

sell, yes sell, all of the merch she had acquired over the years.

I found it hilarious that she had no issue passing on the sinfully stained merchandise of As Cities Burn to someone else, as well as MAKING MONEY off our beer-drinking, cigarette-smoking, devil-worshiping, hellhound heathen asses. If she really wanted to denounce our evil ways she would have gathered some of her youth group friends and held a prayer circle and lit a bonfire to which she would then set ablaze the tainted merchandise that was weighing so heavily on her soul. No shit, when I was in 8th or 9th grade one of our Sunday school teachers organized a bonfire for people to come burn their secular CD's. I did attend, out of peer pressure of course, but I only brought some shitty cd's I didn't care about...maybe The Rembrandts' LP (well-known for the Friends' theme song). Smashing Pumpkins, Weezer, Bush, Oasis were safely hidden away in my CD case. Christians are weird, huh?

A few years later I saw this same girl, drunk off her ass at some bar in Little Rock. We made eye contact that night. It was an awkward moment, as if the tables had turned. Here I was judging HER. She knew it, too. I don't know if hypocrite is a fair word to use. She was just young and stupid before. Then she found out how fun it was to do bad things and probably felt pretty stupid about her email while wishing she had all those cool T-shirts in her wardrobe. This is an example of how difficult fans can make the life of a band, especially for a band that is perceived to be a "Christian" band.

I want you to imagine how fucking difficult it is to try and fit into a thousand different people's version of Christianity. Each member of As Cities Burn differed greatly from one to the next in regards to spirituality and theology. Sure there was plenty of common ground, but no real way to all be 100% behind every single action, thought, or word spoken by any one member of the band.

I mean, even just consider where I'm coming from as a drummer. I didn't write any of the lyrics. I quite honestly don't know what a lot of the songs are actually about, and I don't really care that much. I mean some of the songs "speak" to me sure. But they aren't my words. I play the drums. Kids say things like - "Your songs changed my life" - or "I didn't commit suicide because of your music".

*I wasn't trying to change your life. I was trying to change mine.*

When you gain notoriety, people start to look at you as role models, but they do that through their own lens of what they believe a role model should be. Add religion into the mix and it intensifies exponentially. Fans have their version of Christianity, many times which has been curated by a sheltered, unrealistic world-view facilitated by their parents or their youth group pastor. Then they take this and apply it to the bands they love. When the bands fail to fit into that box, the fan feels betrayed and thus retreats into their bubble and sells - or burns -merchandise and CD's.

We aren't talking about Michael Vick shit here. As Cities Burn was never involved in dog fighting or sex trafficking or some awful action that is universally thought to be despicable and immoral. We're talking about cussing and drinking.

I could never possibly count the times that somebody has commented on Facebook saying something like "I thought you guys were Christian." This usually comes after we post a pic of us all enjoying a beer in a pub in the UK, or today for instance, I posted a blog I wrote that had some evil bad curse words in the headline and throughout the article. And since in some people's version of Christianity, cursing and drinking is no doubt a sin, As Cities Burn's faith is called into question. THE WHOLE FUCKING BAND'S. Based on a blog I wrote. Based on TJ smoking a cigarette. Based on Cody writing lyrics about a relationship instead of The Lord God Almighty.

I hope some of these fans have read this far into the book. I want them to read this. I need them to read this. Do you have any idea the toll this can take on a band? It's soul-crushing. Especially when, in the case of As Cities Burn, we are being totally open and honest. There is no façade. There never has been. Go read Cody's lyrics. They are littered with references to doubting his faith and issues of sin. As Cities Burn wasn't writing praise and worship music to be sung in your bubble on Sunday morning.

Every band that is even remotely associated with "Christian" music has dealt with this, some more than others. If you are open and honest about things, you get the brunt of it. Meanwhile there are massive Christian bands that conceal a multitude of things to save face so they can be paraded around to churches and festivals and provide the safe entertainment for youth group kids. If somebody did an expose documentary about Christian music and the skeletons in the closet of the industry...well let's just say we would see some crazy fan shit go down once the youth groups found out that one of the prominent Christian singers of the last 20 years has been concealing his sexual orientation.

Fans, short for fanatics. That's where the crazy comes from, I guess. It's probably unfair to the majority of music lovers, particularly those who love As Cities Burn. The awful fans stand out more than the cool ones. I'll say this...if you have made it this far into the book you probably fall into that cool category. Hell, even if you hate me now after reading this, you bought this thing, which means I fucking love you. Because what's the point of fans if you can't make money off of them!

# | 11 |

# U-Hauls, Subways, Sodom & Gomorahh, Supermodels, The All American Rejects and Hurricanes: A Tour Story

**It is imperative that a band** does whatever it takes to get to a show. There is no good excuse for missing a show. Ok maybe if one of your members ends up in the hospital after swallowing gasoline, but other than that you better make it to your show somehow. Especially when given the opportunity to open for a band that is blowing up and you hope they one day take you on tour. DON'T MISS SHOWS!

In our case, that band was Underoath and we were supposed to be playing first at their show in Nashville in the spring of 2005. But there we were broke down on the side of the road somewhere in Alabama, still about three hours away from Music City. This show was a big deal for us. Underoath was on the verge of absolutely blowing up, and being label mates and all, there was a good chance that we could land a tour with them down the road.

The show was already sold out, and according to Rado there was already a line forming down the street outside the venue, which at the time was called Blue Sky Court (now The Rutledge). Shows like this weren't the norm for us at this point...well, not in cities outside of Louisiana that is. We were well on our way to being on time for load in as we always were. Punctuality is important when you are at the bottom. DON'T MISS SHOWS AND DON'T BE LATE. Please take note up and comers. But sometimes you are late, because sometimes your van breaks down. Not only did ours break down, it was done. For good.

While we are on subject of what not to do, don't play over your set time; don't break down your drums on the stage. Get moving and get your shit off so the next guy can set up. Don't touch the other band's backline; don't break shit that isn't yours; oh and DON'T PLAY OVER YOUR SET TIME.

We liked having a conversion van. Those bucket seats were damn comfy. And the track lighting, oh boy, I tell you… if we were the womanizing type they (the women) could have never resisted that track lighting. Sexy. Especially when the 12-pack of bottled piss scattered across the floor of the van. Because on tour, one must often relieve themselves into a plastic bottle while the van barrels down the highway at 70 mph. Whenever you think of chicks digging band dudes, is this something that comes into consideration? I don't think so.

Seeing as how there aren't vans for sale on the side of the Alabama interstate, we had to improvise. We had to get to this show. In comes the U-Haul truck. We left the van and trailer (a conversion van with a 5x8 trailer is what we referred to as a "rookie setup") on the side of the road and loaded up our gear and merch in the back of the U-Haul.

Three of us had to ride in the back with the gear. I know Cody and I were back there, can't remember who else...maybe Blake our fill-in bass player. It was a long, dark and hot ride up I-65 in the back of that truck. We had the cargo door slightly open to allow for a breeze to sneak in, as well as enough light to at least see our hands in front of our faces. Assuming this was against U-Haul policy, we were badass and didn't give a damn. We spat in the face of U-Haul policy. Real rock star badass-ery.

Pulling up to the show with hundreds of kids outside was kind of awkward. They seemed to think that we traveled this way by choice. That this was our thing. Touring in a U-Haul. I shouldn't have been surprised.[10] Kids can be pretty stupid. When I say kids I don't mean seven year olds. I'm referring to people that go to hardcore/scene shows. So fans. I guess I mean, "Fans can be pretty stupid."

I don't remember if anyone in Underoath was particularly impressed with our set, but I would guess that they had to respect that we did what it took to make it to the gig. Any hardworking band can appreciate that. The next day we bought a Ford E-350, our first of two 15-passenger vans As

---

[10] *Once a kid at a show asked me if we had "...driven all the way to Wisconsin for just this show?"*

Cities Burn would own throughout our career. It's a staple in the band world. Almost every band has had one, except for the assholes that go straight from nothing to touring in a bus. I feel sorry for them, being deprived of the van experience. It builds character. Buses build egos.

Record release week came at us fast. After the Underoath show we embarked on a four-week small market tour just to stay busy. We were all about staying busy at this point. Home sucked. Tour ruled. We got back to Louisiana only a few days before our big record release show. Colin's parents threw a great white trash themed cookout in their backyard the day before our release party show. Colin was already rocking some sort of euro trash mullet so he fit right in. The girls wore daisy dukes and everyone was covered in American flag apparel. The trashiest thing you can do is wear something with the American flag on it.

By the way, a cookout is what you do when you are grilling burgers, hot dogs, sausages and things of that sort. Not a barbecue. Barbecue is a food group referring specifically smoked meats. In some places like the Carolinas and Arkansas for instance, Barbecue or BBQ (or however you want to spell it) is synonymous with pulled or sometimes chopped pork (either shoulder or whole hog if they are really doing it right). Barbecue is not something you do with your friends on Saturday afternoon or when you tailgate. That's a cookout, bitch.

Friends and family were so excited for the release of our record. It was crazy to think back to our early touring experiences, when everyone probably thought we were wasting our time. Now here we were, a full two years after I joined the band, on the verge of releasing a record on a label we all dreamed of being signed to. The party was much deserved. This accomplishment was worth celebrating.

We kind of broke one of our own rules for the record release show, booking it at a local church in Covington, on the North Shore of New Orleans. It was the only room we had access to that was large enough for what we were expecting, and they were letting us use it for free, basically. Honestly, this is an example of church economics that really bugs me. If you are a Christian and you make art or perform in some way it shouldn't be supported just because you are Christian. Often no weight is put on the quality of the content. It's a big reason I don't like to play churches. It feels fake. Like we didn't earn it.

The plan was to give a CD to every single person that walked in the door. In our record deal we automatically got something like 500 CDs for free from the label. After that they cost us $5 to buy from them. The show was $10, and you got the CD when you paid to get in. This was an attempt to maximize our first week's sales reports to Sound-Scan (a company that keeps track of how many records a band sells). First week sales were huge and could be crucial in shaping the record cycle from that point forward. So it was very important to make a big splash.

The trick with our little plan was that you had to advertise it correctly in order for SoundScan to count it. You couldn't say, "$10 show and you get a free CD." It had to be the other way around. Technically, the kids had to pay for the

CD and then us have the show be free. It's all semantics, but those were the rules. Amazingly, over 800 kids showed up to our release show in Covington on June 21, 2005. By far the biggest draw we had ever seen for an As Cities Burn show.

The next night in Little Rock at Vinos we had almost 500, a sellout for that venue. I grew up going to shows at Vinos, and here I was, my band selling out the club just like Further Seems Forever or Pedro the Lion or Relient K. Dreams were coming true. We had a couple more release shows with the $10 for a CD/Free Show. I can't remember where now. Maybe Nashville. All in all we reported over 1,500 "live scans" to SoundScan by the time the week had come to an end.
      Records are always released on a Tuesday, which means we had to wait until the following Wednesday to find out our first week numbers. I remember being confident that we would break the record for biggest first week for a debut album on Solid State Records.[11] The Chariot was holding the current record with like 4,500 first week sales (I never thought of that as a normal debut seeing has how Josh Scogin had considerable notoriety from his time in Norma Jean, but I digress). We would have broken that record too, but SoundScan gave us an "I don't think so" on the 800 we sold at the church show. For some reason, you can't report scans

---

[11] *In case I haven't clarified yet, Solid State and Tooth and Nail are basically the same. Solid State is the imprint they release heavy music on. Sometimes they release a band on both. We were officially on Solid State. It's a branding thing.*

if the show took place at a church. Probably has something to do with the bullshit economics of the church. Thanks a lot church.

Officially we came in right around 4,000 records sold in the first week. With those 800 from the big release show we would have been the biggest debut release in Solid State Records' history. Whatever the case, almost 5,000 kids had purchased our record in one week. I know that may not seem like a lot to those of you who don't know much about the world I am speaking of, but for a debut album, it was a very strong number. Within a month we would pass the 10K sales mark. Things were moving along.

———————

Cornerstone 2005 was a very different experience than our first time, just a year prior. Instead of a 10 a.m. set with modest attendance, we were playing around 5 p.m. to a packed tent. The best part was we had a record out so there were actually some kids who knew the words to the songs. It wasn't totally insane with kids freaking out. I had to check old YouTube videos before I wrote this section, as to not embellish on how great Cornerstone 2005 was. You can see on the videos that the crowd was relatively mild with a handful of HXC let-me-know-when-the-breakdown-hits-so-I-can-mosh dickheads. But, the tent was full.

Cornerstone 2005 introduced a different type of festival fun to As Cities Burn. This fun included booze, pool parties, hotel rooms and other bands on the fest. Most bands don't stay on site, so we figured out what hotel some band friends were staying at and followed suit. Think Christians gone wild. Some people were even so bold to drink on site at the festival. I can't say I never sipped on a bottle of whiskey in the back of our van behind the stage. It felt so good to break the rules. You'd be surprised how many people performing at Christian festivals aren't even Christians. Some of them were there just by circumstance, as in they just happened to be in a band started by a Christian singer or something, and they were just along for the ride. Some of them were fully aware that they were marketing themselves to a Christian market, even though they had no current affiliation with the faith in their life.

I can't blame them. If I wasn't a Christian, I would start a Christian band so quick. Since there would be no conviction about selling a product in the name of God, I could freely make millions without any repercussions to my conscience. The joke would be on the wacky youth group kids and their parents. But alas, I am a Christian and have resisted the temptation to sellout to the Christian music industry. Mostly.

The rest of our summer would be spent opening for Dead Poetic, another band on Tooth and Nail that was doing well at the time. This was a great tour to go out and promote the new record. Coast to coast, lots of great venues, and we had some really cool people on the tour. The Beautiful Mistake and Classic Case also took part, and although I haven't kept in touch with a single person from that tour, it was definitely about as good of a hang as we ever had. Nobody was big enough at that point to come off as a diva. Every band was traveling in vans. It was kind of an even playing field and quite eventful for us, as well.

Gosh, if you are a fan of As Cities Burn reading this, I really hope you aren't waiting for the moment that I finally dive into talking a lot about this show or that show. I must keep reiterating that there is very little about the actual shows themselves that would be interesting to read about. You want a breakdown of a day in the life of a band on a van tour in 2005? Fine...

Depending on how far away the next show is, we would wake up around 11am each day. By noon we were on the road in search of lunch. Out west, this meant In-N-Out Burgers or burritos. Every day. In the south BBQ was naturally a popular choice. Texas: Taco Cabana! Northeast? Pizza, I guess. Then to the gas station to fuel up, take a piss, and maybe load up on snacks and soda for the drive ahead. Load in time for a show was usually two hours before doors opened, so 4 or 5 p.m. was typical. On the drive I would usually watch a DVD (Freaks and Geeks, CSI, The O.C., Band of Brothers). Cody was a reader; Colin and TJ were usually riding up front and driving, goofing off and speaking a secret language, "DIS DOOD. THA GUY. DIS GUY. SILLY SLAPPY." Gibberish. On this Dead Poetic tour we had Blake our fill-in bassist, probably napping or looking out the window, thinking about how he is 17 years old and a FATHER. Crazy shit.

Nicknames are made up on these drives. I received the name Darren Stains for some reason. No idea why. It was a play on Goldman's studio buddy, Troy Stains. But I don't know why I was branded Darren Stains. They thought it was funny, that's for sure. I mean, Darren rhymes with Aaron. Darren Stains is my twitter handle now. It was probably only funny because of the tone they would use when they called me by that name…similar to on *Seinfeld* when Jerry would call George "Biff". My editor has told me I have to chill on the pop culture and *Seinfeld* references. Here's a suggestion, go watch all 180 episodes of *Seinfeld* and then come back and read my book. Not interested? Well I think *The Purpose Driven Life* is free of *Seinfeld* references, so go have a fucking ball.

Load in consists of just that… loading in your gear. You have to wait to load your gear onto the stage depending on when you are playing. Headliners go first and do whatever they want for however long they want, because they are the headliner. Then main support had their turn, and so on. Then you wait. Maybe sit in the van and chill. Set up a lawn chair in the trailer. Converse with your tour mates. Eat food. Some venues provide dinner, usually bad spaghetti or pizza. Or bad Chinese. The best is getting a meal buyout though. Basically you get $10 from the promoter and then you can go eat as you wish. If you do it right you build up a little stash of cash to lose in Vegas or green room dice games at some point on the tour.

Doors open, kids pile in and we all wait some more. You play your set, load out and pack up the trailer so you don't have to worry about it later. Then it's just party time, drinking back stage or meeting with friends at a bar in the neighborhood. After the show you hang out and sell your merch for a while (or if you have a merch guy on tour with you, they do it while you keep drinking at said neighborhood bar). We'd pile into the van and search for after show grub (once again, In-N-out, Mexican, etc.) As Cities Burn would usually stay with a friend or some fan we met at the show. We might not get to where we were staying until midnight to 1 a.m. or later. If staying with a fan, shit gets weird real quick.

Sometimes they want to show you their music or just keep you up all night spilling their heart out. Fortunately I'm a dick and would just find my way out of these situations and go to bed. Sorry, Cody and Colin. If no fan punishers are present (punisher is what we call fans that just don't understand "the line"), you could wind down, take showers, watch a movie, or just pass out depending on how much drinking had occurred. Then wake up, and do it again. That's van touring in a nutshell. Bus touring is even less interesting than that if you would believe it. Less weirdness occurs with fans on a bus. Easier to escape.

---

I haven't mentioned Tim in a while. This is a great spot in the story to update you. After Welton, Tim had joined up with a band from Wisconsin called Number One Fan as a keyboard, guitar, and auxiliary percussion player. They were getting on some pretty decent tours in early 2005, one of which was opening for The All American Rejects. As described earlier, people easily took a liking to Tim, and AAR was no exception. They wanted to add somebody to play all that random shit for their live show. So while Tim was playing with Number One Fan, he got offered a promotion to come play for a platinum selling artist. Of course he accepted. Over the course of the summer, I would watch my friend Tim play on David Letterman, Jimmy Kimmel, MTV and a multitude of other appearances. ALWAYS wearing an As Cities Burn shirt, mind you. I'm telling you, he was our biggest fan. Constantly trying to push us forward in any way he could. It was very cool to watch. I can honestly say that I was genuinely happy for him and never harbored a shred of jealousy or envy towards his experience. We were both doing cool things in music. That was all either of us cared about. If anything, I was really glad that I wasn't doing better than him career-wise. Tim had severe depression issues, and had been suicidal in the past, before we were close. It made me happy to see him happy.

Tim was really cool about bringing me along to fun things he got to do. Before we both went out for tour that summer, back when I was going to New Orleans a ton while waiting on the As Cities Burn record to come out, Tim came down to see AAR play at HOB New Orleans. Of course I was his sidekick for the night. Per the usual I felt extremely uncomfortable with my surroundings. AAR were actual rock stars. They looked wayyyy cooler than anybody in As Cities Burn. Tyson, the singer, was an actual model, I think. His girlfriend was the supermodel Kim Smith. She was in N'Sync's "Bye, Bye, Bye" video and an Aerosmith video, I think. More on her later.

　　We all went out after their show, and I got really

drunk. Being new to that whole thing, I was a pretty lousy drunk. I talked way too much about a lot of things, including the whole "I can't feel may face" stuff that I had declared during my first drunken go-around in the Vieux Carré.

At one point I said in a fumbling manner to Tyson - "Dude... two years ago I was at Juanita's in Little Rock alllll "swing swing swing" and now I'm like here drinking with you, bro!"

"Yeah, cool man," he replied.

Despite these events Tim continued to show faith in his dumb, uncool friend.

He got As Cities Burn passes to come hang out at Warped Tour on an off day we had in Portland. I tried to stay away from The Rejects this time around, being slightly embarrassed from our previous encounter. I had been receiving reports about how Thrice was the most badass band on earth from Tim. He was right. We also watched our eventual good friends in Emery play on the Smartpunk stage. They were all wearing space suits. Goofy fuckers.

A few days later As Cities Burn was going to be in LA at the same time as AAR. The Rejects were playing a private radio show at Disneyland. Tim got us passes. We were promised a ride on Space Mountain after the show. We waltzed right into Disneyland after the park was closed and proceeded to an underground green room where AAR, along with supermodel Kim Smith, were enjoying some pre-show hangs. I hated every second of it. It was incredibly unnerving to me being in the same room as her. She was perfectly friendly and all that. I believe she was from West Texas, a nice small town girl who now graced the cover of Maxim magazine wearing virtually no clothing. I felt like a 12-year old, crumbling at the knees. We were the same age. The power of a supermodel is devastating to young sexually frustrated band dudes.

AAR's drummer Chris greeted me like an old friend, pointing out that I was indeed much quieter than the last time I had seen him. We lingered awkwardly in the green room for a bit until it was time for the show, which was even more awkward than our green room hang. Being a private radio show, there were only about 300 people there—all teenage girls. The stage was a gigantic Mickey Mouse head, and the band rose from below on hydraulic platforms. AAR must have been compensated well by the radio station to endure such torture. $30K to $60K wouldn't surprise me one bit based on info passed along to me by Tim regarding the absurd amount of cash flow for a band at that level. Nobody got to ride Space Mountain; Tyson was very upset about this, like it was the only reason he agreed to play the show or something. We spun on the teacups or something, I think. I can't remember. All I know is that Chris and I rode one ride together and I continued to be awkward.

After that we crashed at Tim's hotel room on Highland Blvd in Hollywood for a few days, unbeknownst to AAR. Dude was always taking care of us, never worried about awkwardness or consequences. So As Cities Burn experienced a bit of the true rock star lifestyle vicariously through Tim Jordan.

After LA we spent a regrettable 24 hours in Vegas,

arriving in the middle of the night only to have lost more than half my money before the sun even came up. Shows in Vegas were always awful, but boy was it fun to be in Vegas with tour mates. I vividly remember "White Russians" being a popular cocktail on this tour. Of course in Vegas, at the craps or blackjack table, drinks are free. What an awful drink to have many, many servings of. Should have just eaten 'shrooms with Classic Case and walked up and down the strip.

The drive through the desert from Vegas to Phoenix is a great metaphor for the reality of a dumbass band dude leaving Vegas. Having gambled away all my per diems and buy-outs I had saved up, my wallet was empty. A once lush and growing eco system of tour money, now desolate and empty. Depressing to not know how you are going to eat for the rest of the week. Fuckin' Vegas, man.

The tour had made its way back east. We had a day off before our show on Long Island so we called up Mike Watts to see if we could crash at the studio. Plans were made to embark on a night out in NYC. No stretch hummer, just the Long Island Railroad at our disposal. I was boasting with confidence as I had made out with a random girl a few nights before in Virginia Beach. Again, not something I'm proud of, but it's the truth. White Russians make you do crazy things.

My newfound confidence was slightly derailed in Jersey, when a girl we stayed with insisted she was a hair stylist and proceeded to style my hair into that of a medieval Page Boy. You know the look…straight across bangs, but not like a bowl cut, kind of fluffy and curvy around the sides coming from the top. This was definitely not a "relevant" styling in 2005. Who knows nowadays? I mean the "top bun" is a thing that grown men do now. Maybe I should bring back the "Page Boy." Trendsetter baby.

Our good friend JP was on tour with us working the merch table that summer, and he did a fine job saving the day with some electric clippers in the studio bathroom. I was locked and loaded. Ready for the Big Apple. Even had one of those black military-style button down short sleeve shirts from Urban Outfitters that had the cool things on the shoulders. I just asked my wife what they were called. I googled it, too: nobody seems to know.

There were no specific plans for the city. We did know that we would head to the Lower East Side and hit the bars and eat pizza on multiple occasions. And that's what happened. We stumbled across a bar called Cheap Shots on 1st Avenue, a dive bar. I would frequent this place over the years for some reason. You could drink for free on your birthday, but I've never been there on my birthday so who cares I guess. It was just a great bar though. Affordable and lively, lacking pretension, which in New York City is a rarity. Once I stopped into a bar to grab a Budweiser and upon receiving my bill I come to find it was a $10 Budweiser. Insane.

The night slipped further and further into a blissful state of drunkenness and we stumbled out of a bar at closing time only to run into Adam Lazarra, the singer for one of our favorite bands, Taking Back Sunday. He had been having a good time of his own, so when we literally bumped into him he was quite cordial as we recognized him and began to try and convince him to come to our show the next night. Being from Long Island, he was of course familiar with the venue in Farmingdale that we were playing, though I doubt he knew who our band was. Needless to say, ole Adam did not come to our show. Pretty sure he was about as drunk as we were, so maybe he didn't remember.

After another round of garlic knots and slices of pepperoni, we began to make our way to a subway station to grace Times Square with our presence. On the way, walking through the side streets of the Lower East Side, TJ came up with a game that simply consisted of running at full speed and diving into piles of trash. It must have been garbage pickup day the next morning because the sidewalks were lined with massive piles of trash bags. And for whatever reason we thought it was a great idea to throw our bodies through the air and land deep within the mounds of waste. I love how stupid we were. I would never do that now, but I also have no chance of ever having as much fun now as I did then. Youth and stupidity is to be cherished!!

Times Square is only great if you're drunk, or maybe on drugs. I wouldn't know about the drugs part. Well there was this one time many years later when...well, let's leave that for book number two (When Shit Gets Shitty...Part Two). Bubba Gump Shrimp, Ruby Tuesdays and other abominations of dining own the tourist mecca that is Times Square. You all know this. If you are spending a lot of time in Times Square on your trips to Manhattan I just feel sorry for you. But if you get drunk and go there? Bravo. Have yourself a day.

I've been talking about getting drunk a lot in this chapter. To reiterate, I was new to the whole alcohol game, so cut me a little slack. I was doing at 22 what you were doing at 16, except it wasn't at a bonfire at some kid's farm on the outskirts of town. I had the whole world at my fingertips and a group of other young 20-somethings who were down to rage every day. It was awesome. I would learn my lesson by the end of tour though. Later on the tour in Milwaukee, I had no idea that you can't just drink ten pints of beer. My understanding was that ten beers were equal to like three amaretto sours. They're not. I first puked into a urinal. My face IN the urinal.

Colin carried me out on the sidewalk where I puked some more while a group of our friends stood over me in pity and laughter. I puked out the window on the way home to the apartment we were crashing in. Once we got there and realized we were locked out, I made myself at home in the bushes and puked some more declaring, "GOD IS PUNISHING ME!!! IT'S SODOM AND GOMORRAH!! FORGIVE ME O' LORD..." and basically continuing to quote Old Testament scripture. I wish I could tell you how long this went on and give some exact verses I may have quoted, but I was really fucked up and naturally, I don't remember. Where is Welton and their video camera when you need them?

The guys eventually got me into the bathroom where I would get to know the toilet seat quite well, all the while having my band mates answering nature's call and pissing over my head. Fortunately, they set me up with a nice pillow on a tile kitchen floor to spend the rest of the night. No blanket. I haven't been perfect but I can say I have only had this experience three more times in the ten years since, but never this bad. So I suppose you could say I learned my limits.

On this NYC excursion, the plan was to catch a train back to Mike's studio when we were done partying. We hit the subway to make our way to Penn Station. I was leading the way since I was the de facto navigator of the band. Magellan was another nickname of mine. I was like fucking Rain Man with maps and things of that nature. "Follow me guys, when I say this is our stop, get off the train," I said.        "Ok this is our stop...let's go!" I proceed to exit the train. My band hesitates.

　　The subway doors close shut. Colin, Cody, JP, and TJ (Blake was underage so we left that dude at the studio) are standing in the doorway, staring at me with wide eyes and open mouths as the car begins to head down the track. I now stand completely alone in the subway at 4 a.m. in New York City. Not everyone had cell phones in 2005. Definitely not ones that would work underground. Sidekicks were popular with band dudes but they don't work in a subway. I think I probably even left my phone at the studio. Why would I need it, right? I waited. I didn't know what else to do. I couldn't take another train and try to find them. What if they were coming back? I couldn't go on without them either. They didn't know where to go.

　　Finally about 15 minutes later, a train comes in on

the other side of the tracks. As the train departs I hear screaming..."AARON!! AARON!!"

They proceed to tell me that when they got to next stop, they hopped off, rushing to figure out a way to get on a train headed back the other way. A homeless midget approached them and asked if they needed help. They apparently informed him that they needed to get back to the other side and he says to them, "Follow me. Step where I step." The homeless midget took them down on the subway tracks and crossed over to the other side. Sounds like a recipe for disaster, no? Drunk band kids following a homeless midget across deadly train tracks in the middle of the night. Somehow they missed the *third rail* and survived, which is good because this book would get dark a lot earlier than I would have hoped. This is still the fun part.

We made it to Penn Station only to find that there wasn't another train to our destination on Long Island until 8 a.m. A transit cop gave us the rundown of our options, the best of which seemed to be to take a train to the Jamaica Station and transfer from there. Mike Watts had told us, no matter what you do, do not get off at Jamaica. The night was already filled with dumb ass decisions so why not one more? On the way out to Jamaica, we met some real New York girls. I'm talking Long Island native Jewish girls, ya know? Real *Seinfeld* shit.[12] One of our band members decided to

---

[12] *If you remember the lady on Seinfeld who kept telling Jerry and Elaine "YOU GOTTA SEE THE BABY" you can get a good picture of the crew of girls I'm talking about.*

swap spit with one of these girls for reasons I do not understand. I'm not gonna mention who. This is the only instance
in this entire book that I am censoring the identity of an action of a band member. But he knows who he is. We give
him shit about it to this day.

Sitting on the platform awaiting our train to take us further
east into Long Island, the sun begins to rise. This is when
you know your night has really turned to shit. Seeing that
sun come up really fucks up your buzz and puts life in perspective. You immediately realize your entire day will be a
waste. Fortunately we were in a band and didn't have anywhere to be until 5 p.m. that evening. The next train got us
closer to the studio, but still about ten miles away. It would
take a $60 cab ride to reach our final destination. Everyone
was sober by then. As Cities Burn and our buddy JP finally
laid our heads to rest around 8:30 am. That's what I call a
night out in the city. One of the best nights of my life, I
guess. Why else would I remember it in such great detail

Our summer would come to an end with an opening spot for
Evergreen Terrace, a real hardcore band. They had stories of
fights, throwing bricks through windshields of ex-girlfriend's
cars, and other bands they had toured with taking promoters
to the ATM with a gun held to their back to enforce a guarantee. It was a short tour, and it doesn't seem like a band we
would get along with but those dudes were cool. Real nice to
us and didn't give us too much grief for being Christians. We
only had a short break, about a week or two before our fall

touring schedule started up. But we weren't able to go home. We sat in the living room of Lucas' (our new fill-in bassist) parents house and watched as Hurricane Katrina had it's way with the gulf coast.

As we all know now, it wasn't the actual Hurricane that really fucked up New Orleans and the surrounding area. The levees broke and began to flood a city we loved. Cody and TJ's mom had trees coming through her roof, Colin's dad chainsawed his way into his sister's neighborhood to make sure she and her husband were safe. The poor were forgotten and the entire nation watched as the most vibrant and unique city in America went to waste. I remember us all feeling a bit helpless. You couldn't travel down there at that time. There was no fuel to be had and we would have never made it back out to meet up for our next tour opening for Emery. That may seem selfish, but we still had a job to do. So we went up to Arkansas and lived as "refugees" at my parents' house for about a week until it was time to hit the road again.

     I have mixed feelings about not being there to experience Katrina. It truly was a dangerous time in the region, so I am partly grateful that we missed it. On the other hand, I sometimes wonder if we should have done more to get back to family and friends. Even our good friend and recent merch guy JP was displaced. The Best Buy he worked at was shut down and he had evacuated to Baton Rouge, along with the rest of New Orleans. It was a crazy time that we only experienced from afar, watching every day on CNN and trying to grasp the weight of it all. I don't want to be overdramatic, but Katrina probably was the beginning of a strain that was put on As Cities Burn, a strain that would only increase over the coming months. A fantastic summer had come to a somewhat tragic end. Yet we headed into the fall with momentum and upside abound.

As Cities Burn would be on tour for the next 16 weeks without a single day to spare. Seeming so badass to be booked up like that, it was the beginning of the end. Even though the end was technically years away, this balls to wall, don't look back touring hurt our chances for a long career. The future of the band was in peril due to our own ambition and work ethic and a certain disregard for relationships back home, a lesson that would have to be learned the hard way.

# | 12 |
# Touring Ourselves to Death

**Tours are planned really far ahead.** Some big artists—

say, a country singer—will have an entire year or two
planned out to the day. It's not quite that extreme in the in-
die/hardcore world, but I would say around July of 2005, we
knew that we would be on the road pretty much every day
for the rest of the year. After Hurricane Katrina, we were
slated to open up for Emery's headlining tour in support of
their new record, "The Question." Gym Class Heroes and a
band from Seattle called Gatsby's American Dream were
also playing. A very eclectic tour including Hip Hop, Post-
hardcore, Screamo and whatever the hell Gatsby's was supposed to be.

A full US tour for bands like us consist of roughly
40 to 45 shows over the course of about six to seven weeks.
Not many days off and lots of tough drives once you head

west. The drives get especially tough when the headliner is in a bus, because they don't really give a shit how far it is between shows. A professional driver is getting them there through the night while they sleep. That driver makes about $250 per day, unless there is an overdrive contract (say over 500 miles or something) then he makes another $250. This is a small price to pay for the convenience of safety and comfort.

The shows on this tour were really amazing. Emery was blowing up at that time. I believe "The Question" would go on to sell close to 200,000 records[13], which in our world is amazing. Many of the shows would sell out and since Emery was on our label and the fan base was similar, we made out really well on that tour. I specifically remember in Pomona, CA, at The Glasshouse we broke $3K at the merch table for the first time. Mind blowing. We didn't even know that was a thing. Literally four months earlier we were lucky to break $500. That's what having a record out can do for you.

Pascal still had not come back to join the band, yet somehow I guess he was still technically a member. To be fair, he did get hit pretty hard by Katrina. He lived in Metarie, LA, which was heavily flooded when the levees broke. So it made sense for him not to rush to get back on

---

[13] *To put that in perspective for you fans...you think Emery was big? Underoath broke 500,000 records sold for "They're Only Chasing Safety" AND "Define the Great Line." So they were more than twice as "big" as Emery, record to record.*

the road with us. Aside from Katrina, though, I still don't think there was any clarification as to his status in the band. He had been gone through the release of the record and all the touring thus far in support of it. It sure as hell didn't feel like he was in the band. This meant we still had to have a fill-in. Blake wasn't really working out. We all really loved him as a kid, but he was just that...a kid. He had turned 18 just that summer, so we had Colin fire him. Colin always had to do that sort of dirty work. He's tall and intimidating so we figured nobody would fuck with him.

In comes Lucas. He had played bass for a band we were buddies with from Ft. Worth, called Letter Twelve, later changing their name to Terminal when they signed with Tooth and Nail (then many years later some of those dudes would start a band called Oh, Sleeper).

Lucas was a cool guy and all, but once you get in a van with somebody you start to figure out whether or not that relationship is going to work long-term. I admit I can be difficult to get along with. I am heavily opinionated and a little neurotic. Costanza Syndrome constantly makes its way to the forefront of my human interactions. (For reference and a visual example of "George" Costanza Syndrome watch "The Chinese Restaurant" episode of *Seinfeld.*) However, I knew fairly quickly that Lucas wouldn't be around for too long.

When you are a member of the band, it's pretty much understood that if you want to have your significant other come out on the road for a bit, that no permission is necessary. Being on the road and away from your girl is tough. Sometimes this absence really slows down the natural progression of a relationship. In my case, I started dating a girl when I first joined ACB in 2003. We stayed together for 18 months. A good 14 of those months probably saw us on the road. When we were home in Louisiana, she was living in Nashville going to school. So needless to say we didn't see each other much. Looking back, I am certain that if I hadn't been a touring musician, that relationship would have ended in like six weeks. Instead, my absence made it take 18 months to figure out we shouldn't be together. Somehow, I was able to get her to break up with me. Conflict avoided!

If you are married, you basically have carte blanche. There is no limit to the amount of time a wife can come spend on the road, as long as there is room in the vehicle. Now what if you are a fill-in? Should you have to ask? I think so.

Lucas informed us that his girlfriend whom he had only just started dating would be joining us for three weeks. THREE WEEKS. That's almost half of the godforsaken tour. No girl had ever come out with us for that long. The general rule of thumb in my opinion is that once you get past the two-week mark, you are in serious jeopardy of that relationship going down the shitter. I've seen it happen many times. Guy brings his girl out on the road for too long, and then she goes home early without a boyfriend. Boy, have I got a story for you...

Lucas's girlfriend, let's call her Brittany (that might actually be her name, but I can't remember) hops on the tour when we pass through Dallas. Brittany gets up two hours before the rest of us to get ready. Brittany wears a thick coat of makeup on a daily basis. Brittany is a living, breathing Glamour Shot. She always wore a fleece Victoria's Secret PINK jumpsuit. Always freshly tanned. Always freshly perfumed. And always highlighting her massive fake boobs with V-neck shirts under her jumpsuit. I referred to her as like a white J-Lo. I'm not trying to be mean…I'm just trying to paint a picture. She's just typically not the type of girl that band dudes are into. It was just…weird. Apparently I was way off the mark as far as what band dudes are into. I suppose, to be fair, band dudes and non-band dudes alike are into girls with big tits who have no problem showing them off. I mean I was 0% attracted to this girl, but Lucas was not alone. Oh no. J-Lo was getting attention from another guy on the tour.

This all came to a head on the Jersey Shore, about a week and half into Brittany's tenure as a member of the As Cities Burn entourage. One fateful night, Lucas opened his Side-Kick (it was a phone with a keyboard) to see that Brittany had forgotten to log out of her Myspace. Her message inbox was open and there he found a handful of messages that Brittany had written and received from the singer of another band on the tour. Ok, I guess I have to name the band. Because if I don't I am vaguely incriminating Toby from Emery, Travie McCoy from Gym Class Heroes and TJ from my own band. It was the singer for Gatsby's American Dream. Apparently they had taken a liking to each other and were using Myspace to flirt while sitting at the merch table next to each other.

They never had a chance to act on their passionate

online affair, because dumbass Brittany left her inbox open on her boyfriend's phone. How messed up is that? Out on the road with your man for a few weeks, and you're gonna plan a hook-up with one of his tour mates? This was indeed a first. Never heard of it before then, and haven't heard of it since.

Lucas confronted her in Asbury Park, NJ, and informed her that she would have to go home. YESSSSSS! A family friend was going to come pick her up and take her to the airport.

Now I am ashamed to say it, but obviously this was major tour gossip. Everyone was talking about it. So when the time came for Brittany to be sent away, we all made sure we had a nice view of the action. Fortunately, Emery had a bus. Buses have tinted windows. Half the tour got in the bus and watched out the window as Lucas and his love said goodbye. They hugged, reflected on their meaningful relationship (I'm assuming) and continued to hold each other. Brittany's ride pulled up. She began to pick up her things and load them into the trunk. She took one last look over her shoulder, blowing a kiss. A long look of regret and plead for forgiveness. The car pulls away as Lucas gazes into the distance. Then slowly, he begins to slide down the poll he was leaning upon. Closer and closer to the ground, he inches ever so dramatically. Eventually collapsing to the ground, head in his hands in despair. His love, J-Lo, was gone forever. The presumed future mother of his children had taken her jumpsuit and oversized sunglasses to return south, back to the heat of Texas. They would never figure out a way to reconcile and continue their romance.

Am I an asshole if I tell the truth and say that I laughed? I did laugh. Come to think of it, this is the second time I have not been able to hold back laughter at the expense of somebody else's shit situation (the Pascal/Gasoline incident). But funny is funny, right? You can't help it if something is funny. What would you have me do? Lie about it now? I still laugh about it to this day. Don't take it the wrong way. It's not laughing at somebody's pain. I just couldn't believe how dramatic two real life people could be. I wasn't alone. I wasn't the only one in amazement. This was a great moment in tour history. I won't name names, but I PROMISE you I wasn't the only one on the bus laughing. The burden of guilt is with many on that matter.

Other than that, the Emery tour was just great. I even rode on their bus one night from Atlanta to Little Rock (well the bus broke down in Memphis and Tim came and picked me up so I could spend our day off hanging with our friends in Arkansas). That night I rode on the bus with Emery, I got to witness some things that aren't necessarily too awful to write about, but might get me in hot water with the people who are paying for the printing and marketing of this book (Matt and Toby…of Emery).

One thing I can tell you is that their monitor tech, Logan, almost flew through the front of the bus windshield when he was drunkenly stumbling through the front lounge as the bus driver hit the brakes rather sharply. Logan barreled from the bunk area all the way through the divider between the front lounge and driver area and tumbled down the stairs towards the door. Its one the funniest things I have ever seen in my life. I would pay every penny of royalties I accrue from the sales of this book to obtain video footage of this occurrence.

Those dudes were some of the most fun to tour with: dance parties on the bus, hilarious conversations. It was such an encouragement to get to play for so many kids every night and to sell lots of merch. I could probably keep writing about life with Emery on the road but then all those stories would trump all the ACB stories and make you wish I had written about them instead.

It felt like we were still making progress. Our record was selling well and the label was still very stoked on us. We were officially becoming rising stars of Solid State Records. Things were just great. What we should have done was gone home at the end of that tour which was the first week of November 2005. But no, we were road hogs. He had to say yes to everything. We finished the Emery tour and the very next day started in support of The Chariot. Not even a day off to drive.

This tour would take us around the US one more time for the next seven weeks until Christmas. Seven weeks until a break. One interesting development was that Pascal came back. We showed Lucas the door and basically begged Pascal to return. Surprisingly, I was quite happy to have him back on the road with us. We hadn't sounded as good live since he left. He was a good bass player. Way better than Blake or Lucas. Miraculously, he and I were actually getting along. We also added another player to the group to sling merch for us. A strange fella from San Diego named Brendan. We would affectionately come to know him as "Ferg."

Years later this dude would introduce me to my wife (the good one that is...the one I'm married to now and made babies with).

Hardcore tours can really take a toll on you. This Chariot tour was all heavy. Evergreen Terrace and a band called Underminded were the other two support bands. The music is taxing on the ears. I couldn't handle watching many shows on this tour. Maybe we were just tired, but after coming off of such a badass tour with Emery, this tour felt like work. For the first time, I remember not feeling excited to be on the road. I kind of just spaced out for the duration. There were nice moments. Definitely a feeling of solidarity rose in our band due to the mutual disdain for the style of music and types of kids that typically went to these shows. All the dudes on the tour were solid to hang with and everything. It was just an attitude problem on our end.

---

Our touring for the year wasn't quite over when The Chariot tour had run its course. We had agreed to do a four-show run with Underoath, mewithoutYou, and The Chariot. Chad Johnson had organized it as some sort of mission outreach. He called it the "Come and Live Tour." The shows would be huge because it was a great bill. We would have been really stoked to be on it if we hadn't been so worn out. I remember sitting at a pizzeria the night The Chariot tour ended in Atlanta, just totally zoned out and mumbling to Cody about how life didn't make sense anymore. I was too far gone from any normalcy to even hold a conversation with someone I wasn't on tour with. There were a ton of friends and even kids from the show at this pizza joint, and the idea of talking to any of them was torture. By this point, the idea of talking to even my own best friend was something I dreaded.

Towards the end of the summer of 2005, Tim returned from a European tour with All American Rejects to learn that he was being fired. The band sat him down in a hotel room in Seattle, with a plane ticket home to Little Rock. I'm not sure how specific they were with the reason, but it was done. He was devastated.

Tim had been going through a lot that summer. He had been involved in an extremely co- dependent relationship with a girl from Little Rock. He found out she cheated on him while she was studying abroad for the summer. The day this news came to light, we talked on the phone for hours. I remember I was in Philadelphia on tour with Dead Poetic, drinking a Yuengling and eating a roast beef sandwich at a bar with a bunch of dudes from the tour when I got the call. He was hysterical and crying about her, telling me all about the infidelity. It was awful. But what made it even more difficult was the fact that I knew he had cheated on her with multiple girls over the previous six to eight months.

Knowing Tim, it was totally understandable why he was reacting this way. He was an emotional dude. But knowing that he had cheated on her as well, it was truly bizarre that he was reacting this. I'm sure somebody that knows about psychology could diagnose this for me. I don't know much about it. Throughout the remainder of my friendship with Tim, I would learn more and more that I didn't know anything about how to deal with what he was going through.

After he was fired from AAR, he returned home with basically no prospects in the music department. I was hoping he could come out and join ACB, but before that even came to be a possibility, our good friends in Jonezetta snatched him up. We had played a small roll in Jonezetta getting discovered by Tooth and Nail in 2003 (or, a year after we signed). Our manager Ryan Rado ended up managing them as well after we insisted that he come inside and watch their set once when they were opening for us in Monroe, LA. Then he pitched them to The Nail and voila!

They signed for an insane amount of money for a new band with no sales history. Jonezetta had wanted to add an auxiliary guy to play keys, guitars, percussion and sing background vocal parts. Welp, I called up Robert Chisolm from Jonezetta and told him about Tim. I was finally was able to return the favor to Tim, hooking me up with As Cities Burn. Next thing I knew, Tim was hosting Jonezetta at his lake house in Camden, AR, writing songs for their debut record. Good matchmaking, Aaron. Way to help out a friend in need! The problem was that all the things that were haunting Tim during his tenure in AAR just carried right over into Jonezetta. While I'm out on the road getting my ass kicked by a brutal touring schedule that consisted of living in a van for a span of 34 weeks STRAIGHT, I'm also working damage control for my best friend. On The Chariot tour, when playing at The Door in Dallas, TX, I received a call from Tim after we had already played our set. This was pretty damn close to the end of that tour, maybe a week left or so. I was beat.

Tim was crying, saying how he didn't want to live anymore. He was so upset I could hardly even make out what he was saying. I didn't know how to help him. I was so exhausted; I didn't even feel like helping him. That's the honest to God truth. I had nothing left to give to anybody. You may think that sounds terrible. But unless you have experience with someone who is suicidal and dealing with very serious mental issues, it may be hard for you to understand how unfair it is to the person that is burdened with the weight of being the one who has to help. Feeling that if I didn't do something he would kill himself was too much. The pressure of, "You better say the right thing right now or your friend is dead," is not something that a normal person knows how to deal with. I was 22 years old, a stupid kid who loved my friend. But I didn't know how to help him. I kept telling him, "I'll be home soon, man, and we will work through this shit. Just hang in there." I was tired and wanted to go walk with my band to get a slice of pizza. But there I sat, on a sidewalk in Deep Ellum, listening to my friend sob.

Let's go back to that night in Atlanta, sitting with Cody in the pizzeria totally zoned out and exhausted. It was December 12, 2005. We would crash with this Asian kid who literally went by the name Brian Asian (later known as Ping, he would end up working as a guitar tech for Anberlin and Thrice). The next day we were going to have to drive to the mountains and Alabama for the "Come and Live Tour Retreat". All the bands were meeting up for a couple days before the shows to do retreat-type stuff. Bible studies, worship, prayer, charity work: it's basically the worst nightmare for someone like me who has social anxiety extending into spiritual social anxiety (i.e. I hate praying out loud in public).

Sprawled out on the living room floor of a strange kid who openly embraced somewhat racist nicknames, I crashed hard when my head hit the pillow. Maybe around 4 a.m. that night (now December 13) I heard my phone ringing. I picked it up to see that it was Tim calling. I knew in that instant, that if I picked up the phone I was signing up for a sleepless night of consoling a guy that was claiming to be on the verge of suicide. What did I do? What any good friend would do. I went back to sleep. I would just try and call tomorrow.

The next afternoon, walking around the mall in Douglasville, GA, I tried calling Tim over and over. No answer. No returning my calls. I felt guilty about the night before. I kept trying and trying. Nothing. I left one last voicemail telling him that we were headed into the mountains for the retreat and I may not have service, but to please call me back when he can.

At this point I was really worried. I mean, I know you may be thinking I should have already been worried, but Tim had been threatening suicide for years before I knew him. His mental health issue ran deep into his past. He was always able to pull through. I figured he was just in a really bad spot because of everything going on with his girlfriend. But now I couldn't get a hold of him. That wasn't normal. We talked in some form almost every day while I was on the road. Not about just serious stuff. Shooting the shit about the road and whatever else was going on was a daily occurrence. Now here I was about a week after he told me he wanted to end it all, and the day after I ignored his 4 a.m. phone call, unable to get him on the phone.

That night at the retreat, I felt some really weird shit. Like spiritually. It was around 8 or 9 p.m. during a worship service at this cabin we were all staying at. Already, I didn't want to be there due to being road-weary. My attitude about the whole thing was shitty. And the stuff with Tim, it was weird.

During the worship service, I swear it felt so real. A darkness came over me; it felt like it came over the entire room. I'm worried some of you are thinking, "Ok this guy is going off the rails now…what a wacko." That's fine. I don't blame you. I do sound like a lunatic right now, for sure. Even sitting here typing, I'm hesitant to go forward with this section. Partially because I sound crazy. And partially because every time I talk about these moments in that cabin, it takes me to a place I don't want to be. The room felt engulfed in this darkness. All around me I sensed evil and despair. Tragedy. I swear to you, I knew in that moment.

I couldn't sleep that night. I was up all night in the bathroom dry heaving. I thought maybe I was getting sick. Colin had come down with some sort of really bad cold or flu and we were in the same room.

The next morning, everyone from the tour was supposed to get up and go build houses for Habitat for Humanity. Colin and I stayed behind. Not long after the cabin was empty, around 7 a.m., I received a call from a friend of mine. Her voice was quivering.

"Aaron, are you sitting down?"

"Yes..." the anticipation was too much to bear. I knew what was coming.

"Tim killed himself last night."

His plan was for his girlfriend, who shall remain unnamed, to find him. They had been fighting that day, and he insisted that she come down from Little Rock to Camden (about two hours south of Little Rock) or he would kill himself. Not that there was an outcome that would have been better or worse, but his father, who loved him dearly, was the one that would find Tim, hanging in the closet of the lake house. The coroner said it was sometime between 8 and 9 pm on December 13. The same hour that was the darkest, scariest of my life during the worship service in that cabin. I left tour that day and flew home to Little Rock to be with friends. Life would, of course, never be the same.

I don't remember the last conversation I had with Tim. I only remember the one I chose not to have with him, the one that could have happened less than 24 hours before he took his own life. Thinking back to that night, sleeping on a living room floor ignoring a desperate phone call from the most loyal friend I have ever known, I am overcome with guilt. Every time. All those months of touring and success were now completely meaningless to me. In my mind–at that time–it was because of my choices and touring schedule that I wasn't able to be there for my friend. My lifestyle had rendered me too selfish and too tired to pick up the phone at 4 a.m. when Tim needed me most. My world was shattered, and Tim's ashes were spread over a lake in Camden, AR. No going back. No "I'll call you tomorrow, buddy."

# | 13 |
# Soundtrack

**On the road, music was everything.** When you tour in a van, you have countless hours throughout the day to fill as you traverse across the United States or worse…Canada. I hardly listen to music anymore, and I definitely never discover anything new these days. But during my touring days, music kept me going. Music, kept me inspired. A band dude cannot survive on *C.S.I.* episodes alone. This is a look into my soundtrack for touring.

**Sigur Rós "Takk"**

Riding on the back bench of the van, we were heading north on the 101. On my left I see the ocean in the distance. On my right, mountains and rolling hills dominate the landscape. This is the beauty of California. I've escaped from all thoughts and pressures of a tour. It doesn't matter how long ago since my last shower, or how much money I have in my wallet. In these moments on the most breathtaking stretch of highway in America, I feel the presence of something beyond my physical existence. It might have been God. Or maybe just adrenaline. I have a hard time believing it wasn't God. Riding along, admiring the complexity and unlikelihood of the way the earth had settled, how could it not be proof of a master creator? A perfect design.

There was something propelling these feelings of the metaphysical and thoughts of existentialism: the heavenly sonic waves traveling from my headphones into my ears. Sigur Rós was taking me closer to God than I have ever felt inside the walls of the church. With lyrics that are said to be gibberish, the music can mean anything to anybody. It's a brilliant endeavor, leaving nobody out, except those imbeciles who may despise the sound of what I can only describe as a sonic nirvana. The songs make your life into a movie of sorts. Cameron Crowe understands. He must feel what I feel, because he masterfully inserts the wonder of Sigur Rós into his films. In the soundtrack of my life, no other makers of music have inspired me and carried me through a multitude of life events, joyful and devastating.

The experience of watching them execute their brilliance at The Ryman Auditorium in Nashville, TN, on Valentine's Day 2006 will stay with me 'til the day I die. I was standing at the top of the balcony, considering all the possibilities for success or failure in multiple facets of my life. Dealing with the loss of a friend. For two straight hours, I was constantly on the verge of tears. So much change in life. So much hurt.

## Jimmy Eat World "Clarity"

I'm sitting in the driver's seat of our old conversion van. It's winter in Chicago, January 2004. This was the night As Cities Burn decided to record a new demo, the demo that would eventually land us a record deal and take us to new heights. Conversations of refocusing and doubling down are an inspiration. A record I had been told over and over to fall in love with, but had yet to give my attention to. This night, "Clarity" would receive all the attention, and all of my love that is possible to give to a single record.

I already loved Jimmy Eat World. "Bleed American" was a staple in my rotation. I was a bandwagon fan, I suppose, jumping on after "The Middle" hit it big. I didn't care though, because it was such a great record. The real fans would tout "Clarity" though. That was the masterpiece. It had nothing to do with cool. It wasn't that Jimmy Eat World had now made it onto the radio. "Clarity" was different. It was modestly produced. The songs made you feel uncomfortable and happy in a way that's not ideal if your goal is to sell two million records. The "real fan" were right.

Diving into this record, I thought maybe the CD was broken. I kept turning the volume up as I saw the seconds ticking away on the player. Finally, the soft sound of a Leslie organ begins to sustain. Ride cymbal and snare softly make their way into the mix. No bass drum. It's so important to notice that. Go listen and observe the restraint by Zach Lind to leave out the bass drum. Then while still so quiet, the verse starts over with the bass drum hitting the down stroke with the bass and acoustic. A shaker sounds in the background. Never building. Never getting louder. Jim Adkins executes masterful but almost elementary harmonies. When the chorus hits, it's powerful and unsuspecting. It's as if only one more instrument came into the mix, but the display of dynamics leading up to that moment created a climax that many bands are too impatient to wait on.

Every track is a home run. Jimmy Eat World is by far the most frequently played artist in my iTunes.

**Death Cab For Cutie "Transatlanticism"**

Sometimes a record comes along and causes you to think about music in an entirely different way. I could never describe to you the context of that statement now because I am in an entirely different state of mind artistically since when I first heard this record. I have had an entire decade of art and life experience to influence my musical point of view since then.

But I remember the moment, in Madison, WI, touring with Welton and my friend Tim. Talking in the van after a show and traveling across the same winter roads as during my gushing of love for "Clarity," we're completely engulfed in experiencing this record. The sound engineer had begun the record over the venue sound system after the show was over. Standing there, I bask in the emotions that the unassuming voice of Ben Gibbard can stir up. With lyrics so clever, running deeper than an ocean trench, I said to Tim, "This changes everything for me."

## Nada Surf "The Weight Is a Gift"

It's 6 a.m. and Tim wants to show me new music. I hate being shown new music. I love to be told about new music and then possibly fall in love on my own time. But Tim wanted to show me…at 6 a.m. on the way to Philadelphia after an all night drive. He was riding along and offered to drive. And since he was my best friend, I was expected to ride shotgun. With the sun coming up, and me being pissed off at the world just for being awake, Tim blasted this record. I hated it.

I regret not learning to love Nada Surf while Tim was still alive. I owe him so much in regard to the records I love. After his death, I would discover that Nada Surf is my favorite band. They're so bravely simplistic. Never straying from what they do well. You could call it a lack of artistic progress. I simply believe it's doing what they do well. Their records could pretty much interchange a bunch of songs at random and totally make sense. I'm totally ok with that.

The narrative on several of the tracks paralleled so much of what I felt during the time after Tim's death. Happy sounding songs for the most part, but their lyrics punched you in the gut with a dose of reality.

"Maybe this weight was a gift. Like I had to see what I could lift."

Ain't that the fucking truth.

**Kevin Devine 'Fingerprints and Photographs'**

I feel bad when I don't get into an entire record. Picking out a single song to love seems cruel and unjust to the work the artist put into the entire record. But this was the case with this song.

The Arkansas countryside is simply amazing. There's so much to appreciate once you stop hating a state that felt like a third world country compared to where I was born and where my beloved Braves resided nearby. Dragged away from the land I loved, my family settled in Cabot, AR, when I was 12 in January of 1995. The Braves would win the World Series ten months later, and I would resent the Natural State throughout my formative years. Having left to join As Cities Burn, I had time to let appreciation grow. This song captured those feeling perfectly as we navigated our van through the back roads of Southwest Arkansas, leaving behind a girl and her parents' farm. I always knew this relationship would never work out, but it took a year and half to end.

Watching the cows, observing the fields and a signature Arkansas sunset, this song took me to a place of appreciation. Arkansas was poor and way behind the curve culturally. And there was no Major League Baseball team. But it was beautiful. Most importantly the people there are beautiful. I have no family there anymore, but I will always long for that feeling I had listening to this song, passing through the fields of a state much looked down upon. I love you, Arkansas.

**mewithoutYou "Catch For Us the Foxes"**

This was the first record I feel like all the members of ACB fell in love with simultaneously, while on the road together. I believe we first popped it into our CD player in Jackson, MS. It was 2004 and if memory serves me correctly we had just opened up for Norma Jean at a church. This was yet another one of those records that was something so unique and daring, something I had never heard anything like.

I hate spoken word. I hate most things vocal-wise that aren't singing. Aaron Weiss wasn't singing, but he wasn't just speaking either. It was a perfect marriage of two ends of the spectrum. And where the vocals lacked in carrying an actually melody, the guitar work picked up the slack. For a band seemingly so outside the box, both artistically and in the personalities they projected, they had a pop sensibility surpassed by nobody in our scene. And the drums, oh the drums...

I have been on tour with mewithoutYou and we have loads of mutual friends. We were label mates. Living in the same world. But I've never spoken a word to anyone in the band. I'm that intimidated. And now it would be just so awkward to finally introduce myself. Ugh...

**The Cardigans "Long Gone Before Daylight"**

Once again, I have Tim to thank for the delight and depression this record has contributed to my life. Once again, I didn't get into it until after Tim was dead. In a lot of ways this record really helped screw up my life even more. The emotions I was dealing with in the period after Tim was gone led to the most fucked up relationship you could imagine, and records like this perpetuated the delusions that would eventually contribute to my demise. If only I could have just been satisfied with falling in love with Nina, her soft and soaring melodies. I could have avoided a lot of heartbreak. Damn you, Tim.

**Phantom Planet "California"**

It all comes back to California for me. It's the happiest place. I loved it so much I ended up moving there and meeting the love of my life and mother of my children. I got myself a California girl. But this isn't about a Katy Perry song. This is about ACTUALLY cruising down the 101 jamming to this song. We all loved it. We all sang it out loud. On tour, California is the Promised Land. Perfect weather. Badass shows. And massive, cheap burritos.

It's so difficult to capture the essence of a place in a song. Few have done it better than Phantom Planet. Just take me to the beach, man. Let's build a bon fire and grill some carne asada. Also, I FUCKING LOVE AVOCADOS. Good choice, *The O.C.,* for making this your theme song. I watched that entire first season in 36 hours. That's the kind of time you have on tour. You watch *The O.C.* non-stop, dreaming of the next time you return to California. God Bless this liberal wasteland of overtaxation, drought, and absurd real estate prices. And God Bless you, Phantom Planet.

# | 14 |
# Breaking Things Up

**In the days and weeks after Tim's death** I was quite
somber and composed. I seemed to find myself in the position of consoling many who weren't as close with Tim. I
didn't mind. It was my way of dealing with it, I guess. The
idea of playing a victim and constantly being sad and putting
the weight of my suffering on others around me was repre-
hensible. Tim had done that to me. I didn't hold that against
him, but I didn't want to do it to others. I didn't really care
about my band anymore. We had a tour coming up in February, but I dreaded going back on the road. I wasn't sure
how I was going to handle that grind in the emotionally
volatile state I was in.

     Everywhere I went, I wanted to fight somebody. I
never did, but it's all I thought about. I was angry at any random person I interacted with. Angry that they had no idea

what I was going through. How dare they, right? When I'm ordering my coffee at Starbucks, you better acknowledge that my best friend just committed suicide. How could you be so insensitive? Baristas ought to know better, right?

In the same way that I wanted to fight everyone, I had no care or respect towards anybody outside of my group of friends. Since the world could not understand my pain, I gave myself a free pass to proceed as I wished. This led to me straight up pursuing the girlfriend of a guy who was in a band on our label. She lived in Little Rock, and we been friends for quite some time...ever since she dated Tim years before.

    For two years she had been dating a guitar player from Haste the Day, a band that had tried to help us get noticed by Tooth and Nail. Years before, she did make the first move by telling me she had a crush on me. After Tim was gone we found ourselves out drinking, as we quite often did in those days. She joined this time and informed me that the crush still lingered. I would soon declare my "love" for her and go down a path that would destroy her current relationship and eventually lead to a disaster of a relationship of our own. It's almost as if you shouldn't make big life decisions or "fall in love" a couple weeks after your best friend kills himself.

    None of it was worth it. I hurt a really good guy and would pay the price with years of misery and heartache. December of 2005 through summer of 2009 is a book all on its own, without any mention of a band. That relationship was a train wreck from the beginning. My friends knew it. I didn't listen. Maybe one day I will write about all that. Not yet though.

---

Our next tour was another hardcore tour. I pretty much couldn't stand to listen to any of the bands for more than a few minutes. A band called The Bled, from Tucson, AZ, was headlining. I just looked up the dates and it was a 44-day tour that started in Seattle and ended back in Tucson. That's brutal for a band from Louisiana. That meant we are driving cross-country to begin and end the tour. So basically it's a 50-day tour. Which based on everything you have read so far, isn't abnormal. But everyone in the band was affected by Tim's death. Everyone was close with him (except for Pascal). Everyone loved him. And as I've stated before, Tim was our biggest fan. It hit hard and a 50-day tour that never quite clicked for us was a recipe for failure.

Fans of The Bled weren't really into us. I don't think The Bled really cared too much for us, either. I kept my distance from pretty much everybody, spending most of my time watching DVDs in the van or just hanging with the dudes in my own band. Apparently I was so unknown on that tour, that several weeks into it, I was unrecognizable to this guy Ross that played guitar in The Bled. We were hanging at a party after our show in Dallas (I believe it was at James from Oh, Sleeper's apartment), and I was talking to Ross about touring and things of that nature. The conversation proceeded to go like this:

Ross: "Oh cool man, what band are you in?"

Me: "...Ummmm, As Cities Burn? I'm on tour with you..."

Ross: "Wait...oh gosh, I'm sorry man. Yeah, yeah..."

He had no clue who I was! I really want to write LOL and HAHAHA right now. Is that ok? Pretty funny, I think. Also it's a testament to just how disconnected I was on that tour. I had realized about halfway into the tour that I had not met nor spoken to    The Bled's tour manager. I figured it would be a fun little game to see if I could keep that going for the rest of the tour. I was successful until after the last show. For some reason he hugged me and told me goodbye. That's a tour thing: saying bye to every single person on the tour and maybe doing a "tour picture" which sometimes can involve upwards of 25 or 30 people. I have since learned to avoid this and virtually say no formal goodbyes to anyone. I'm much happier this way.

Sitting down at a restaurant somewhere in the middle of nowhere (possibly in Canada), As Cities Burn decided that we were going to call it quits. Everyone just seemed kind of miserable. TJ had decided that he was going to get married and didn't want to tour anymore. The dominos fell from there and we all agreed we should end As Cities Burn. It wouldn't feel right to go on without TJ.

Our summer was being planned during this time. So far we were booked to support Underoath in May and then head straight into a three-week stink on the Smartpunk stage on Warped Tour. Then we would do our first real headlining tour that would be our "farewell" tour. We had been touring for just under three years at this point and were throwing in the towel. Thanks a lot, Tim. Way to break up my band with your poorly timed suicide. Hey, dark humor works for me, so deal with it.

Talk about some badass shows, that tour with Underoath in May 2006 was freaking ridiculous. Remember how we sold $3K in merch one night on the Emery tour in Southern California? Now we were doing that almost every night in places like Tulsa, OK. Absolutely insane. The biggest show on that tour had something like 3,000 kids in attendance. It was like playing the tent at Cornerstone every night.

Many nights were spent at bars after the show, listening to Aaron Gillespie and Spencer Chamberlain trying to convince us to stay together. "We'll take you guys on tour all over the world," they said. Breaking up was a foolish thing for us to do according to anyone on the outside looking in. I was starting to agree. We were having so much fun and making a lot of money. I was still hurting from Tim but as it tends to happen, time was healing. The post-traumatic tunnel vision of nothing-else-matters-except-for-Tim's-death was wearing off. I had a chance at a successful music career. We had momentum and a lot of people were saying they were going to get behind us. The label thought we were the next Underoath. The entire summer of 2006 would be spent listening to people trying to convince us to stay together. Underoath, Emery, Tooth and Nail. It was nonstop. One big problem was that it was looking like Cody and Colin already had other gigs lined up. Cody was going to move to Boston and join The Receiving End of Sirens in the fall, and Colin was planning a move to Atlanta where he would join up with a fairly new band called Manchester Orchestra. At that point, I felt like I was the only one who wanted to keep it going. I had no other prospects or opportunities.

I secretly hoped that Jonezetta would kick out their drummer. Based on conversations with Tim and their singer Robert, it seemed like a real possibility. They would end up getting a new drummer, but Jonezetta would fizzle out after their second record. Tim's suicide really did a number on Robert. They were set to go into the studio to record their debut "Popularity" just weeks after Tim's death. Robert was never the same after that. I've lost touch with him for the most part, but other than myself, I feel like he was the most heavily affected by the whole thing. I was just able to handle it a little better. I mean, I messed up my life pretty good, but I didn't get into mental breakdown territory.

———————

Warped Tour sucks. That's not accurate actually. Warped Tour fucking sucks. Before you call me an ungrateful bastard, just go talk to a few other people in bands that have been on Warped Tour. I don't have a single band friend who disagrees with me. Never once have I sat around reminiscing about the good ole days at Warped Tour with an old band buddy. All we talk about is the bullshit. The 7 a.m. check-ins; the pushing our gear to a stage a half mile away through gravel or sand; the lack of air conditioning on our piece of shit bus, that we were sharing with a piece of shit band. There is this saying that Warped is like a "Punk Rock Summer Camp". If that summer camp takes place in hell, on one square mile of asphalt in Phoenix, AZ when it's 120 degrees out, then yes I suppose Warped Tour is like summer camp. Otherwise it's just something you do as a band because you just can't turn it down. It's "bad business" to say no to Kevin Lyman and The Vans Warped tour.

Tooth and Nail put up the money for us to split a bus with Scary Kids Scaring Kids. A few minutes after we all met up and started heading up I-85 from Atlanta to Baltimore, we knew it was a mistake to share with them. First the keyboard player starts jumping around, doing his best impression of a monkey with a top bun. Licking people. Yes. Licking. He hopped right over next to me, squatting with his hands touching the couch in between his feet and just started licking me. Never figured out the reason behind that. Maybe just trying to break the ice? Seems…unnecessary and maybe unsanitary.

Then came the weed. Nobody asked us if it was cool if they smoked weed in the bus. I suppose they just assumed that everyone likes being crammed in a smoke box with 12 other dudes. Surely EVERYONE smokes weed, right? Even the bus driver. He must smoke weed, too! Oh yes he does…while he is driving! Not kidding. This happened.

I don't know much about the herb. I don't have a problem with it, either. But it doesn't seem smart to get high driving a 60-foot bus and trailer while 12 young kids are placing their lives in your hands. Scary Kids didn't seem to care. Come to think of it, they didn't care about a lot of things. Personal space. Fucking random girls anywhere they please, at any time of the day. It was a mess. We weren't a party band. We liked to drink and chill. I didn't want to walk in on the drummer for a band that I absolutely despise musically, balls deep in some 18-year old girl that he just met. Just bummed me out. A couple times we would come back to the bus after our set, sweating our asses off and dying of heat exhaustion, to find just the most insane party going on. Drugs, sex and rock and roll. The real deal. Maybe that's why I hate Warped Tour.

I'm sure our tour mates played a large part in it, but it really was just a big hassle for very little reward in my mind. The shows were pretty good, but not any better than if we were just opening for a cool band. Pretty sure we didn't get paid, and merch sales weren't great. For the bands that are on the main stage and blowing up, it's great. All your gear is on a truck that gets loaded directly onto the stage, and there were reports of bands selling $30,000 of merch in a single day. But even people from those bands would say how much they hated having to do Warped Tour. In that scene it's tough to do anything else in the summer other than Warped Tour. They kind of monopolize the summer. Not being on Warped Tour is kind of being left out of the loop. Out of the cool club. Like I said, even though you might hate it, it's not something you turn down. You just go out and do the work.

Our stint on Warped Tour was only 3 weeks. That was enough for us. We had better times waiting for us. Finally, we had a real headlining tour. We picked the support bands. We get to keep all the money. It's our show, baby. One last hoorah. The "Farewell" tour was well promoted. Even though we had been a band for only a short amount of time, it seemed that quite a few people cared that we weren't going to be a band anymore. Maylene & the Sons of Disaster, Jonezetta and Lorene Drive would join us as we said goodbye to the world forever. It was a great group of dudes to end it all with. We had been friends with Maylene for years before they were ever a band, and of course our history with Jonezetta traces all the way back to my second show ever with the ACB in 2003. At some point during this tour we put together a Creed ensemble and would play a medley of their biggest hits in between Jonezetta's set and Maylene. I sang backup vocals. Mainly the "and I say Ohhhhhhhh" on *My Own Prison*. It was more fun that actually playing our set.

Speaking of our set, we put together a great one, fully taking advantage of all the emotions we could possibly pull out of fans and ourselves. The end of our set was like the heaviest worship song ever, the type of performance that would leave you with nothing left to give each and every night. That was the attitude we had. This was it; let's give it everything we got. This was best displayed on what was to be our final performance at Cornerstone Festival.

There are some great videos out there on YouTube of that performance. We were booked for one of the late night slots, which already just sets up the mood. The side of the stage was filled shoulder to shoulder with friends and former tour mates. For many, this would be the last time to witness As Cities Burn perform.[14]

The outpouring from fans was shocking. We had no idea that our music was having such an impact on people's lives. Maybe it's because we were breaking up, and people just had the courage to say things that they figured they wouldn't have a chance to say in the future, but it definitely had an effect on everyone in As Cities Burn. Night after night, in every city, fans pleaded with us not to be done. Chad Johnson had a serious talk with us one night at Cornerstone about how big of a mistake we were making. Basically arguing that the proof was in the pudding. We were drawing great crowds at every show. The record had sold almost 40K copies in a year and there was no sign of slowing down, except for the whole final tour thing. He asked us to reconsider. It's funny because he told us that while hanging out with our label's owner Brandon Ebel at Cornerstone, they were discussing us breaking up and Chad played a little joke on him.

Chad told Brandon, "Hey, As Cities Burn says they will stay together and do another record, but they want $5,000 each..."

Brandon said, "That's it?!" Should have pursued that probably.

---

[14] YouTube has been a great tool for me throughout the writing of this book. So many old videos of As Cities Burn can take me back to a time period and get my mind right to address a specific event or memory. I encourage you to do the same if ever you are looking for some point of reference.

Standing outside in the back alley of a club in Denver, CO, after yet another amazing show, Cody, TJ, Colin and myself were discussing the future. Everybody had come to the conclusion that we were making a mistake. How foolish it would be to end something this special now, without ever reaching our full potential. It was decided right then and there that we would keep the band together. But without Pascal.

We couldn't quite figure out the best way to tell Pascal that although the band was going to stay together, it would be without him. We were so bad at it that we actually went ahead and announced at our Seattle show that we weren't breaking up, meaning at that point he planned to carry on. I think we were hoping he would quit. I mentioned a bit ago that he and I were getting along better. That didn't last long. Ferg told me that I got out of the van one time at a gas station and Pascal said to everyone, "Before this is all over I'm going to punch that dude in the face." So I guess the feeling was mutual.

I think he thought everyone wanted to kick me out. That he wasn't alone in his desire to, in the words of Buddy Rich and George Costanza, "Take me outside and show me what it's like." Pascal even tried to convince us all that Ferg was skimming off the top at the merch table. We told Ferg about this, and from that day on (well the few days that Pascal had left with As Cities Burn) if Pascal was near the merch table Ferg would very obviously sneak a twenty dollar bill out of the merch money and put it in his back pocket. I would watch him do it. Hilarious. Still a running joke between all of us to this day, along with Lucas sliding down the pole.

In San Jose, sitting in our van outside of the house we were crashing at, Colin led the conversation to kick out Pascal. I strategically sat in the front seat so that I wouldn't have to make eye contact with the dude. And so that if he tried to take a shot at me, I would have a quick exit. Dude was not happy, of course. We told him if he wanted to finish the tour, that was fine with us, or we could get him a plane ticket home for the next morning. He opted to fly home. I've only seen and spoken to him twice since then. That was nine years ago.

Robert from Jonezetta would finish out the tour on bass. He rode in our van the next day on the way to Fresno or some shithole like that out in Central California to learn all of the songs. The next couple weeks would be the most fun I had ever had playing shows with our band, because finally I wasn't constantly annoyed in some way at the bassist. Whether it was his quality of performance or personality, I had always had a problem with my counterpart in the rhythm department. No longer was this the case.

The tour was on the home stretch. What was supposed to be the final shows of our career were now just another step in the path to stardom. As chronicled in the first chapter of this book, As Cities Burn had our eyes set on a sell out of that House of Blues in New    Orleans. Now that we were staying together we were full of hope and excitement for the future. It was all big things from here.

Watch out Underoath. We are coming for you. Watch

out Warped Tour main stage. No longer we will be sharing a busted ass bus with a pothead for a driver. My bank account was going to be increasing exponentially over the coming years. I might even buy a Land Rover like Tim had. And maybe a DW drum kit. Truth Custom Drums will come knocking soon. They didn't want to endorse me before, but you just wait. And when they do I'm gonna say, "Thanks, but no thanks. I have my OWN drum company because I'm rich, bitch!"

But you know how it ends. I already told you. I've ruined the ending for you since the beginning. There are no surprises or twists in the plot. It hasn't been a dream all along. This isn't the fucking *Sixth Sense*. I hope you're not disappointed, because I told you what would happen. I told you it wouldn't get bigger and better. That final show in New Orleans was the top of the mountain. And then next few years, personally and professionally would be a constant state of tumbling down from that peak. That's the damn truth.

# | 15 |
# Unrealized Expectations

**I'm 32 years old.** I drive for Uber to make money for my family. I'm largely unsatisfied professionally. I love my family dearly. My wife, Cassie, is a saint and my kids, Magnolia and Buddy, are truly a gift from God. But I deal with a tremendous amount of anxiety regarding what I am doing with my life. I have burned-out and quit a lot of things: cooking professionally, managing bands, saying I'm going to produce bands and pursue more studio work. I've made plans to try and get gigs down on Lower Broadway in Nashville, playing country covers. I spent a year building a website where songwriters could sell custom songs to their fans, only to have it all fall apart a few weeks after the launch. I haven't followed through on a myriad of things.

When I was in high school I had potential as a baseball player. I'm not saying I was the next Chipper Jones or Greg Maddux, but I definitely could have gone on to play college and with some development, possibly play professionally in some capacity. I was a pitcher. A damn good one. I could throw a changeup and was hitting the mid-80s on the radar gun when I was 15. But I quit that, too. I didn't know that it was anxiety back then. I didn't even know what that was. But I threw in the towel. I don't know what it's about, everything I pursue triggering anxiety. Is it fear of failure? Was I not afraid to fail with As Cities Burn?

I had a previous marriage fall apart. Granted I didn't want to actually get divorced. Technically it was annulled...don't ask me how cause I don't know. She had a good lawyer, I guess. I had no lawyer. I didn't put up a fight. I did a piss-poor job of keeping my marriage together. The same way I did a piss-poor job of trying to keep As Cities Burn together when it ended in 2009 after three years of a steady drop off in fan base, record sales, and income. TJ had gone ahead and quit the band after that summer farewell tour of 2006, and we believed we could be even bigger without him, because screaming means small and singing means big. Shifting our sound to more of a rock/indie vibe was going to be our cash cow. We were wrong, of course.

Even though my previously described selfishness and growing disconnection from my core group of friends played a part in the demise of As Cities Burn, it's the only thing I haven't really wanted to quit. To this day I have done things and worked deals to try and keep it going. We started playing reunion shows back in 2011 and I have been dragging Cody along convincing him to keep going with these cash grabs ever since.

Our first show back was at a big winter festival in Dallas called Unsilent Night, in December 2011. They offered us an absurd amount of money to play, which is why they were able to convince everyone to do it. That day we sold over $16K in merch. One show, $16K. We went to the UK for three weeks in the summer of 2012. We toured with Underoath on their final tour in January 2013. We have fielded a host of other offers that never materialized. Demand has been high. As Cities Burn is bigger now and more valuable than it ever was back in 2006 at our peak.

I am currently organizing a tour to celebrate the release of our first record, "Son, I Love You At Your Darkest." It was ten years ago this summer. I'm still chasing that high. I can't shake the tour bug. I want to be on that stage with Cody, Colin and TJ putting it all on the line, spiritually and emotionally. This tour will make us more money that we've ever made in our lives playing music. But that's not a peak. That is nostalgia.

New Orleans, summer of 2006 is still the top. All the things I am doing now, only involve chasing that feeling again. From my perspective, it's a somewhat sad attempt to capture a piece of my youth. Deep down inside I still hold out hope that there is time for As Cities Burn to make a real comeback. Time to make another record that will be bigger than anything we've ever done. Time to sell out a US tour in 2,000 capacity rooms. Time to tour Southeast Asia and Australia, Germany and Russia and South America. Time to see the world. Time to achieve everything we fell short of.

All of these dreams hold me back from a pursuit of reality. It's the reason I can't commit to another "career." If I hadn't kept getting myself sucked back into making music with Cody on side projects and reunion shows and this and that, maybe I could be a very successful tour manager for a country artist by now, like many friends I know here in Nashville. Maybe I would be a successful chef, with my own restaurant and cookbooks and 100% artistic control over all aspects of my career. Instead, I've moved around looking for the next gig to get me to the top, to attain the success As Cities Burn never achieved. I've been in a band in San Francisco, another in Tampa, performed as a country artist here in Nashville. The dream is alive, but not well.

But I don't want to give up the dream. I hope the tour we do this summer will lead to a record. And I hope that record leads to a release tour. And I hope that tour leads to another ten years of As Cities Burn. Because playing music for a living is a career, in my opinion. You don't have to grow up and get a real job. You can pursue your dreams and find success. But you cannot be afraid of the failure that awaits you. You have to be delusional. Only the delusional ones make it.

As Cities Burn feels unfinished to me. Just like everything else I have pursued in my life. Come to think of it, finishing this book is a miracle. About seven weeks ago I told my wife that I thought I should write a book about As Cities Burn. I started rattling off stories and ideas. I got really excited as I do just about every other day about some new business idea. I never follow through though. She knows me, and I am positive that her only explanation for me actually finishing this book would be divine intervention. Maybe I have found a new career in writing. A career I will actually pursue with fervor and passion. Just like music.

My career as a musician may be one that is envied by some. After all, most people that play an instrument never even realize the dream of going on tour. I at least did that. Our fans love our records. I am really proud of our records in general, especially the last two. The music and career of As Cities Burn has been very special to many, myself included. But that hasn't been enough for me. My dreams are actually unfulfilled. My expectations, unrealized. What we did wasn't good enough. We only scratched the surface of what I believed we were capable of. We let it slip away.

What a luxury it would be to go back to that August of 2006 in New Orleans. Do it all differently. Do it all…better. What a luxury it would be to have answered that phone call from Tim the morning before he decided to take his own life. What a luxury it would be to "know the way it all would end, the way it all would go." Fuck you, Garth. Your song is full of shit.

As Cities Burn fell short. I have fallen short. Sob story, eh? No. I'm happy. I love most things about my life. How many people can say that? But, in regards to As Cities Burn? We fucked up.

So now, getting ready to embark on this nostalgia tour we have a chance to fulfill the dreams of the past. We have our own bus for the very first time. The money we are getting paid to play these days is enough to facilitate the character crushing lifestyle that a bus provides. All the bands that we aspired to be have mostly moved on, broken up, or fallen by the wayside. Maybe they fulfilled their dreams. Or maybe they wanted more. Band dudes are often fame whores. We need validation from the masses.

Tooth and Nail Records is not what it used to be. The "Golden Era" as I call it is over. Underoath is gone. Emery is gone. Norma Jean is Gone. August Burns Red is gone. Anberlin is gone. As Cities Burn…gone. I don't really know who is still on the label, but I would bet none of their current artist are experiencing the success of the "Golden Era". It's kind of like the wild west in the music industry now. There are no rules. Everyone is trying to figure shit out. Nobody really knows what to do or how to do it. Labels like Tooth and Nail are FIGHTING to stay relevant.

As Cities Burn is no exception when it comes to fighting for relevance. That's why we recorded a couple new songs this year. To alleviate just a little bit of the stigma of nostalgia. "Hey! We have something new! Please like us again! Please????" I'm trying not to fuck it up this time around. I'm trying so hard to hold things together. It feels like there is a lot on the line. Reputation, legacy, pride… money. Lots and lots of money. The type of money I always hoped we could make one day. "One day" is here and now I am realizing I am not prepared to handle it. Maybe it was all a blessing, the band falling apart as it did.

By the time most of you are reading this, the "Ten Year Anniversary Tour" will have already happened. You the reader, will have the luxury of certain information I do not currently possess. I started this book writing about how we hit our peak almost 10 years ago. The question is - "Did

As Cities Burn fulfill the expectations of 10 years ago in 2015?"

House of Blues New Orleans is the first show of this tour. The irony. Can we sell it out this time? I have no idea. If we don't I might just quit the tour before it even happens. How much disappointment can a drummer sustain??? I do know this - I will be standing on Decatur St. in New Orleans drinking an Abita Amber while I watch our CREW load in all our gear. For a couple weeks in the summer of 2015 I will have the chance to live out my dream of being in a "big" band.

Did As Cities Burn finally get to go on tour with all the bands we dreamed of getting to share the stage with? Thrice, Thursday, Taking Back Sunday, Coheed and Cambria, Jimmy Eat World and countless other bands were on our list of dream tours.

Maybe we can finally get our name on that wall at House of Blues New Orleans. The mark of a sellout show awaits us. In reality the inevitability of disappointment is my destiny. I'm gonna bet that if you go look up what I'm doing now, As Cities Burn is not in the equation. The summer of 2015 was most likely the end of the line. I hope I'm wrong. Really, I do.

Even if we do sellout that show in New Orleans, I'll keep wanting something more. I won't truly be happy unless every single show of the tour sells out. Satisfaction is not attainable for the hungry. Bad news for me, because I am a God Damned glutton for validation from the masses.

Made in the USA
Middletown, DE
12 September 2015